LIBERAL ARTS AND SCIENCES
Thinking Critically, Creatively, and Ethically

Christopher A. Ulloa Chaves, ED.D.

Order this book online at www.trafford.com
or email orders@trafford.com

Most Trafford titles are also available at major online book retailers.

© Copyright 2014 Christopher A. Ulloa Chaves, ED.D.
Book Cover photograph credit to Mr. John Sequeira

Print information available on the last page.

ISBN: 978-1-4907-3699-0 (sc)
ISBN: 978-1-4907-3701-0 (hc)
ISBN: 978-1-4907-3700-3 (e)

Library of Congress Control Number: 2014909351

Trafford rev. 03/30/2016

Trafford
PUBLISHING® www.trafford.com
North America & international
toll-free: 1 888 232 4444 (USA & Canada)
fax: 812 355 4082

Dedications

This book is dedicated to my mother, the most courageous woman I know, and my father, who was a knowledge seeker and deep reader in spite of the world he grew up in. They both had the courage to allow their children to discover who they are and what they wanted to do in life. As a Presbyterian, I also want to dedicate this book to Fra. Angelico Chavez, an American scholar, poet, priest, and historian of the American Southwest (see http:// newmexicohistory.org/people/fray-angelico-chavez).

Contents

LIST OF TABLES

LIST OF FIGURES

PREFACE

The liberal arts and sciences are the foundation for initiation and development of the free citizen and competent professional in society. When we address the issue of the arts and sciences, we can contrast between Greek and Roman preferences, the world of ideas and the world of matter, or theory and practice. But, it was during my years of teaching university-level courses in learning and teaching theory, the history of higher education, business ethics, and critical thinking that I would discover philosophy's ancient and ongoing impact on the liberal arts and sciences in the West and increasingly so in the East; indeed, ancient philosophical forms and content serve as the foundation for what we know as liberal learning content and methods and, by extension, the humanities and the social and applied sciences.

Philosophy's impact on contemporary liberal learning begins with Socrates's critical analysis approaches, which model how to analyze and evaluate the knowledge we take for granted but also create new understanding; Plato's focus on ideas, justice, and political philosophy; and Aristotle's emphasis on experience, ethics, habit, and logic. It continues with Hypatia's teaching and development of mathematics and philosophy at the Library of Alexandria; Thomas Aquinas's synthesis of faith and reason; Rene Descartes's writings about the nature of reality, reason, and the importance of doubt; Francisco Suarez' ideas on natural or inalienable rights; Immanuel Kant's contribution to social ethics through the *Categorical Imperative*; John Dewey's progressive work on experiential education and education for democracy; John

Rawls's conception of fairness as a form of justice for those in the minority; and Martha Nussbaum's writings on human capabilities and the importance of liberal education to cultivate humanity.

While the preceding list of luminaries is incomplete, the enterprise of philosophy and its impact on liberal learning efforts in the current global commons is indisputable. As we shall see, the discernable objective among these and other philosophers' ideas was the furtherance of human emancipation, development, and the potential for personal fulfillment in life. The pursuit of life, liberty, and happiness, as enshrined within the U.S. *Declaration of Independence*, is one such example of a recent culmination of a forgoing thread of ideas involving Socrates, Aquinas, Suarez, Locke, and Jefferson This emancipation was, and continues to be accomplished, through the crucial relationship between ancient and contemporary philosophical ideas as discussed and engaged within the various formal and informal liberal learning contexts; these contexts can include colleges and universities, professional discussion groups, experiential learning venues, think tanks, libraries, some religious organizations, book clubs, prison education programs, and others.

Often, philosophy, and its progeny liberal education, is marginalized as anachronistic and out of step with the marketplace, religious, and political agendas of the contemporary world. It is interesting, however, that, arguably, the oldest Asian civilization, China, is currently in the process of gradually importing Western liberal educational concepts; it has become obvious to Chinese elites that, for instance, the ancient Socratic tool of critical thinking is necessary in order for assessment and creativity to flourish in their business and research environments. Yet some may argue cogently that while Asian authorities are generally allowing more economic freedom, not much political freedom and social expression has been encouraged of late; and so, it seems to many that exploiting critical thinking's powerful tools, only to realize greater market share gains in a reemerging China, is not an entirely positive development for the transcendent goals of educating the whole person or citizen. Liberal learning stands as a powerful autonomous educational experience, but it requires a free democratic society to enable its beneficiaries to flourish. But as non-Westerners, Chinese elites are choosing a different set of priorities.

On the other side of the globe, Western societies within Western Europe and the United States are in the throes of a macro-civilizational identity crisis. While the West can be credited for the eventual development of political, economic, religious, and social freedoms unknown to mankind previous to the Renaissance, its abuse of the first three forms of freedoms on the world stage, mainly through colonialism, has now undermined its role as a leader of legitimate ideas and philosophies. One might argue that the legitimacy of the very ideas that the West advanced remain so but not its messengers.

However, philosophy and its essential premodern conceptions are not necessarily the brainchild of the current declining power centers of the West. Indeed, the enterprise of Western philosophy did not begin in the western European Anglo-Saxon, Hispano, or French worlds but in the Mediterranean Greco-Roman worlds of southeastern Europe, seemingly at the epicenter of European, Islamic, north African, South Asian, and Russian cultural influences.

Thus, scholars engaged in the education and learning contexts of the twenty-first century must explore, critically analyze, and sustain much of the ancient, modern, and contemporary Western philosophies while also acknowledging the similarities between these and the wider world philosophies stemming from Chinese, Indian, Islamic, Slavic, Meso-American, and African civilizations.

Regardless of its main roots, it seems that in order for philosophy, and its progeny the liberal arts and sciences, to sustain its legitimacy in the diverse contemporary world, it must shed its elite mystique and instead be a salient and respectful Socratic participant in the public and global marketplace of ideas. Without liberal learning, we could not have developed the ability to think critically, creatively, or ethically. Indeed, liberal education models can produce learning, or change, by being one of the key voices which question how the fruits of scientific, religious, and political ideas help, or not, in educating, developing, and sustaining more whole human beings and, by extension, a more just world.

A road map forward

Specifically, in chapter one, a general thematic exploration of how the enterprise of philosophy began and what purposes it served as an early form of educational experience in a free society will be discussed.

In chapter two, a discussion on the roots and value of a liberal arts education, as a form of canonized ancient but contemporary philosophy, are explored in a more historical than thematic fashion. In chapter three, the humanities are explored in their diverse manifestations, as found within formal and informal learning contexts; this chapter makes the case that it is within the humanities especially wherein human empathy can be initiated for others in the world. In chapter four, the major historical and contemporary concepts of what learning is understood to be are explored, in addition to, how learning methods inform educational processes in the classroom or work setting. Chapter five will explore the first major consequence of philosophical discourse, specifically the development and necessity for critical thinking and reasoning in the personal and public spheres of society; for instance, thinking critically about what has gone before us, and what currently is, can potentially help us forge a better future.

Chapter six will explore the concept of thinking creatively as an ongoing intellectual exercise in the research ideal, meaning, the need to expand or create new knowledge and to develop future-centric cosmopolitan thinking. What does it mean to think creatively in the sociological, technological, economic, ecological, and political realms within a closer world scene? Chapter seven will address the issue of normative ethics; among other questions, how can an ethical frame of mind create a more just society for all of its members but guard against self-righteous or dogmatic thinking masquerading as morality? We begin with chapter one involving a thematic discussion on the enterprise of philosophy and its influence on higher learning in the free society moving forward in the twenty-first century.

CHAPTER 1

PHILOSOPHY: A WAY TO HUMAN DEVELOPMENT

The rest of the arts are called liberal because
they befit free men, but philosophy is liberal
because its study makes men free.1

Vergerio (1370-1444)

🦉　🦉　🦉

Defining what we mean when we use the term *philosophy*, and its association with human developmental experiences, can pose a challenge since this term seems to only apply within ancient sociological contexts or be the sole province of the eccentric intellectual who engages in conversation about abstract ideas which seemingly have no genuine relevance to the contemporary world. But if our intent is to begin to discern between truth and falsehood or between right and wrong, then philosophy has much practical value in the contemporary world. While philosophy has been described in many ways, it can generally be understood to involve a love for wisdom, an ongoing exploration for what one considers to be true, and these which inform a certain way of life.

---

[1] Vergerio, Pier Paolo. Character and Studies Befitting a Free-Born Youth. In *The Great Tradition: Classic Readings on What I Means to Be an Educated Human Being.* Ed. Richard M. Gamble. Wilmington: ISI Books, 2008, p. 313-323. Print.

Love of wisdom

Most philosophers and scholars simply define philosophy as the *love of wisdom;* this is usually what the official understanding is for the Western conception of philosophy. This word is essentially a contraction involving two terms, namely *philo* (love of) and *sophia* (wisdom). The word *love* has many conceptions, but as it relates to philosophy, we can understand it as a genuine affection for what is wise in the world; thus, wisdom is the object of our intellectual affections. Wisdom, on the other hand, can be succinctly defined as when a person has certain knowledge "to discern inner qualities and relationships" among people or systems or, described to represent "accumulated philosophic or scientific learning."[2]

For example, Socrates would in one case employ key questions in his attempt to understand the inner qualities or essence of what true piety was. During his dialogue with a religious scholar named Euthyphro on the steps of the king-archon court, the former requests from the latter greater clarity about what genuine piety is, stating that "I did not bid you tell me one or two of the many pious actions but *that form itself* that makes all pious actions pious"[3] (italics mine). For Socrates, it was only in understanding exactly what the inner essence, or definition, of what a pious action was that could give him the ability to develop an objective standard to apply when attempting to discern whether or not a person or a practice is genuinely good.

Wisdom can also be represented as a canon of reliable insights or scientific discoveries that continue to inform new questions or research. Thus, a teacher will use Confucius's *Analects*, Indian *Upanishads*, Plato's *Republic,* or chemical laws like the *Law of Multiple Proportions* to create new learning experiences for her students. So one kind of wisdom is philosophic, and the other is

2   "Wisdom." *Merriam-Webster.com*. Merriam-Webster, 2012. 21 April 2014.
3   Plato: *Five Dialogues Euthyphro, Aplology, Crito, Meno, Phaedo*, 2nd Ed. Translated by G.M.A. Grube. Indianapolis: Hackett Publishing Company, Inc. 2006, p. 8e. Print.

scientific, but they are both strongly desired for their continuing value and potential to inform new understanding in the world.

Many times, however, our insights or decisions are informed mainly by an emotional preference that eclipses the wisdom of logic or basic rationality, as in the case of love for an unreliable person, a material item, or support for a narcissistic and unethical politician. An overreliance on our emotional dimension to make most key decisions can often prevent our cognitive faculties from discerning the true inner character qualities of leaders, social dynamics, or the practical utility of a product or service. It is important to recognize that we or others will use the emotional dimension to persuade us about any number of issues or decisions. Generally, it can be a good thing, I suppose, if some type of balanced influence, involving both cognitive and affective processing, informs our initial understanding or decision making. The need to make wise decisions seems to take priority during a personal crisis in ours or the lives of those we care for; and so, strongly relying upon what we know to be wise, meaning reliable understanding, that we can apply as a way to enlighten our path forward, invariably becomes important to us.

Political philosopher and writer Robert Nozick argues that wisdom represents knowledge and understanding of many facets pertaining to the human experience; he writes:

> Wisdom is not just one type of knowledge, but diverse. What a wise person needs to know and understand constitutes a varied list: the most important goals and values of life—the ultimate goal, if there is one; what means will reach these goals without too great a cost; what kinds of dangers threaten the achieving of these goals; how to recognize and avoid or minimize these dangers; what different types of human beings are like in their actions and motives (as this presents dangers or opportunities); what is not possible or feasible to achieve (or avoid); how to tell what is appropriate when; knowing when certain goals are sufficiently achieved;

what limitations are unavoidable and how to accept them; how to improve oneself and one's relationships with others or society; knowing what the true and unapparent value of various things is; when to take a long-term view; knowing the variety and obduracy of facts, institutions, and human nature; understanding what one's real motives are; how to cope and deal with the major tragedies and dilemmas of life, and with the major good things too.[4]

Nozick argues that wisdom constitutes a multitude of special knowledge relating to the complexity of the human life. He writes that wisdom helps us understand more about key values; what is realistically possible in life, goal attainment, and our personal strengths and limitations; and how wisdom can improve our relationships with others, regulate our motives, and help us deal with life's tragedies should they occur. An ancient example from Plato's dialogues can help us understand some of Nozick's ideas as they apply in the real world.

When we read the dialogue between Socrates and Crito in Plato's *Republic*, where the latter attempts to convince the former to leave Athens before the sentence of death on Socrates is carried out, we can begin to discern how a decision on the part of Socrates to leave Athens can trigger a whole series of related and negative consequences. Benjamin Jowett (2006) translates this part of the dialogue as follows:

'For just consider, if you transgress and err in this sort of way, what good will you do either to yourself or to your friends? That your friends will be driven into exile and deprived of citizenship, or will lose their property, is tolerably certain; and you yourself, if you fly to one of the neighboring cities, as, for example, Thebes or

---

4   Nozick, Robert. What is Wisdom and Why Do Philosophers Love it So? in *The Examined Life*, New York: Touchstone Press, 1989, p. 269. Print.

> Megara, both of which are well governed, will come to
> them as an enemy, Socrates, and their government will
> be against you, and all patriotic citizens will cast an evil
> eye upon you as a subverter of the laws, and you will
> confirm in the minds of the judges the justice of their
> own condemnation of you. For he who is a corrupter
> of the laws is more than likely to be a corrupter of the
> young and foolish portion of mankind.[5]

The consequences outlined above seem to impact on the personal, social, political, economic, cultural, and legal dimensions connecting Socrates, his family, friends, and the Greek Isles. Following through with Crito's advice would trigger what is generally known as an "international incident" with hardly any benefits to be realized by Socrates or his loved ones in Athens. Disliking, indeed hating, what is wise in this important case would create one more Greek tragedy in the city of Athens.

In the end, Socrates would not betray his commitment to the law but demonstrate his love for what was wise in his heart and mind; he would not regress on his professed way of life. He would not allow a prejudiced verdict against him to ultimately discredit, as he believed it, his God-given work as the gadfly of Athens. To Socrates, Athenian culture required deep levels of improvement, and he would accomplish this by entrenching an educational process that involved critically analyzing and evaluating many of the values, attitudes, and beliefs Athenians took for granted. Ultimately, Socrates secured his immortality.

The love of wisdom has moved many to initiate and inform discourse experiences wherein individuals can begin to ask, or engage in, questions and answers about wiser courses of action in life which actually begin to benefit ourselves and those we care for around us. Actually realizing genuine benefits from wisdom then, presumably, develops a strong desire, if not a long-term love, for

---

[5]   Jewett, Benjamin. The Republic Crito Book II. *The Complete and Unabridged Jewett Translation*. New York: Vintage Books, 1991. Print.

wisdom of many sorts in our lives. Philosophy has also created the dialogical vehicle to engage in the search for truth, an ancient description that essentially connotes an educational process.

Searching for truth

Philosophy also can be understood to facilitate a *search for truth*. The act of searching in the intellectual sense generally requires careful and thoughtful study, dialogue, and investigation. Defined in this way, the search for philosophical or scientific truth often begins by engaging in an educational process including the definition of key terms and concepts, key follow-up questions, and an ongoing dialogue which tends to often produce greater clarity about what may be true or not. Merriam-Webster (2012) defines *truth* as "the body of real things, events, and facts." Philosopher and religion scholar Huston Smith posits that truth can be informally defined by each individual as the current reality, the way things exist, or how they actually occurred.[6]

But truth, as beauty, is often in the eye of the beholder. This is perhaps why there can be related but varying accounts made by different witnesses to a particular automobile accident on a busy freeway system. There are both conflicting and related dimensions reported by different people at the same automobile accident. In the Christian Bible, specifically within the four gospels, we have seemingly different perspectives about the life and deeds of the man called Jesus of Nazareth. Indeed, the process of searching and determining what truth can be for a certain context or situation has often been controversial, enlightening, liberating, and occurring for at least 2,400 years in the Western and non-Western worlds; we see this process occurring within many sources, including Plato's dialogues, Cicero's *De Republica,* the Hebrew and Christian Bibles, the Koran, the Upanishads, or in the Confucian Analects.

---

[6]   "The Wisdom of Faith with Huston Smith." Episode 5 A Personal Philosophy. Interviewer Bill Moyers. Athena Learning, 2011. DVD.

The idea of what could be accepted as truth to live by has been different based on certain intellectual emphases. For instance, from Plato's *Theory of Forms,* we get the concept of *idealism,* the belief that the intangible ideas in our minds are the only true things in our world; thus, the fact that our light blue vehicle can be destroyed in a fire does not extinguish the truth that in our Western mindset the color concept of *light blue* is unchanging throughout time or that two plus four will always equal six. Moreover, the form of *beauty* is what can be considered common between peaceful sunsets in a desert, flowers in bloom, or a placid ocean scape. While it has been said that beauty is in the eye of the beholder, it usually cannot be denied that these three descriptions of nature can be a beautiful experience for human senses.

Conversely, those who subscribe to the concept of *materialism* believe as Aristotle that matter, or tangible things, are what can be counted on to be the only true things in this world. While it may be true that two plus four equals six, it is only in physically adding two blueberries with four blackberries that we touch and see that we have six total berries in our hands. Thus, for contemporary empiricists, the search for truth requires the application of a scientific approach or method that serves to explicitly confirm or deny the truth of a hypothesis, an informed idea which must be tested that is attempting to explain a physical phenomenon which may change over time.

Thus, in our current postmodern era, supposed truth claims must be empirically verified in a credible way in order for them, ultimately, to inform courses of action that will impact animals, human lives, or natural resources. Indeed, Yale University professor of medicine Steven Novella posits that, at a basic level, discernible natural effects (a form of truth) must be explained as having natural causes and not rooted in a category of the miraculous, supernatural, or, I might add, the emotional dimension.[7] But do all forms of truth need to be empirically verified?

---

[7] Novella, Steven. *Your Deceptive Mind: A Scientific Guide to Critical Thinking Skills.* The Great Courses, 2012. CD.

For many, the intangible dimensions of emotions or thoughts still carry legitimacy as we know that while thoughts and feelings cannot be tangibly seen, they are nonetheless *real* to individuals considered, for instance, to be in love with each other; for them, it is *true* that their partner's feelings of love are genuine, discernible, and being manifested through selfless or disinterested acts toward each other. And so, friends or family members make life-altering decisions or commit limited financial resources to benefit a loved one or even a stranger.

Thus, idealism, as initiated by Plato, belongs within that branch of philosophy called *metaphysics;* and materialism which often intersects with the scientific method, and necessarily accomplished independent of religious and political authority, belongs to the branch of philosophy called *epistemology,* the term that defines the method which enables us to better *know what we know.*

Whether one determines truth by giving more credence to the ideas in our minds or the concrete experience in the material world, what we accept as being the *truth* usually produces a learning experience in our lives; learning is synonymous with the experience of change in mind, body, or spirit. But for genuine learning to occur, an educational process involving a guide or teacher must be a part of the search for truth.

Plato describes the process of searching for truth or reality in his *Allegory of the Cave.* He describes this search, a form of intellectual development, as a process involving, first, the realization that most of us are born in the cave of intellectual darkness and the passive recipients of illusionary tales and myths delivered by others using, as it were, a movie projector. Plato's cave represents the inside of a modern-day movie theater whereby the film projector above and behind the audience projects various illusionary images onto a screen in front that tends to keep the viewers in emotional infancy and in a captive intellectual state.

One day, however, one of the prisoners decides to leave the cave by ascending nearby stairs that lead up and out into the light of the real world, but it is not all smooth sailing at the outset. Using Jewett's (1991) translation, Socrates explains the experience of discovering the genuine truth of the real world in his response to Glaucon, stating:

> And now look again, and see what will naturally follow if the prisoners are released and disabused of their error. At first, when any of them is liberated and compelled suddenly to stand up and turn his neck round and walk and look towards the light, he will suffer sharp pains; the glare will distress him, and he will be unable to see the realities of which in his former state he had seen the shadows; and then conceive someone saying to him, that what he saw before was an illusion, but that now, when he is approaching nearer to being and his eye is turned towards more real existence, he has a clearer vision,—what will be his reply? And you may further imagine that his instructor is pointing to the objects as they pass and requiring him to name them,—will he not be perplexed? Will he not fancy that the shadows which he formerly saw are truer than the objects which are now shown to him?[8]

It seems that the prisoner who chose to initiate a search for truth, a true educational process, began to experience what we now term *cognitive dissonance*, meaning, there is essentially a conflict between the understanding he has previously acquired and what he now has a "clearer vision" of. Indeed, his instructor is requiring that the prisoner actually name various objects being shown to him and this while struggling with his own doubts about what he already knows or takes for granted; it will require a sense of intellectual liberation and autonomy in order for the former prisoner to confidently name the new objects.

---

[8]   Jewett, Benjamin. The Republic, Crito Book II. *The Complete and Unabridged Jewett Translation.* New York: Vintage Books, 1991, pp. 253-261. Print.

As will be discussed in a later chapter, what we actually have here in this allegory is an ancient description of the goals of a liberal education—basically, that the educational process described in Plato's *Allegory of the Cave* represents the process of human emancipation that often begins during the early years of a college level liberal education program. The student, for instance, has left his small town nature of reality and has walked into a larger social context which will require that he question and shed unexamined views and beliefs and, hopefully, choose to acquire and assimilate better and broader understanding of the world.

However, the prisoners who choose to remain in the cave do not have the benefits of an instructor, an educator, but are forced to teach themselves what the truth may be regarding the objects presented to them on the movie screen in front of them. In fact, Socrates states:

> Being self-taught, they cannot be expected to show any gratitude for a culture which they have never received. But we have brought you into the world to be rulers of the hive, kings of yourselves and of the other citizens, and have educated you far better and more perfectly than they have been educated, and you are better able to share in the double duty. Wherefore each of you, when his turn comes, must go down to the general underground abode, and get the habit of seeing in the dark. When you have acquired the habit, you will see ten thousand times better than the inhabitants of the cave, and you will know what the several images are, and what they represent, because you have seen the beautiful and just and good in their truth.[9]

---

[9]   Jewett, Benjamin. The Republic, Crito Book II. *The Complete and Unabridged Jewett Translation.* New York: Vintage Books, 1991. pp. 253-261. Print.

It seems that by acquiring the habit of seeing in the dark, a genuine sense of illumination and leadership ability in society can be achieved. As the wise owl's ability to both see effectively through the dark and to scan its environment 360 degrees, so can the enlightened individual develop their ability to see through the deceptions in the world and understand issues more comprehensively. For example, it is by first understanding (light) what a genuine dollar bill should look like that one can discern the counterfeit dollar bill (darkness) in the "underground abode." As the search for truth can introduce us to the beautiful, what is just, and good in life, philosophical dialogue also can help us inform and develop a good and flourishing way of living and in community.

A WAY OF LIVING

Philosophy has been explained in such a way as to characterize a *way of life*. Plato's teacher Socrates would be one of the first social philosophers who would demonstrate and challenge us to think for ourselves about how to undertake a way of life worthy not only of a free citizen but also of a just and inquiring individual; it seems that examining our views and hegemonic assumptions pertaining to the worldly dimensions around us, temporal and spiritual alike, would be a central way of accomplishing these personal and social goals. Certain schools of thought in the ancient world were necessary to inform diverse ways of living.

For the ancients, a philosophical school of thought gained notoriety based mainly on its leader's authentic way of life.

Examples of certain ways of living include Socrates's commitment to discovering through dialogue how to live a good life; Plato's emphasis on the primacy of ideas, dialogue, and justice; or, as in the case of Aristotle, direct experience with the material world. According to Oakely, becoming a member of Plato's Academy in Athens essentially involved a "change of heart and the adoption of a new way of life . . ."[10] Later schools of thought informed an Epicurean's belief that increasing pleasure and decreasing pain in life was of utmost importance for the human being or that a Stoic's commitment to being indifferent to what he or she had no control over in life or in relation to others was central to this school's curriculum.

As regards a pre-Socratic school of thought, the Pythagorean way of life, which also influenced Plato, began for most candidates with a requirement to keep silent for up to five years before matriculation into this fraternity could be achieved; only then could a student of this mystery school be trusted with its most closely held secrets about mathematics, metaphysics, and other occult knowledge.[11] Pierre Hadot writes that "the philosophy of Plato—and, following him, all the philosophies of antiquity, even those which were farthest away from Platonism—all shared the aim of establishing an intimate link between philosophical discourse and way of life."[12]

Invariably, if the free human being has the ability to choose their own way of life, then the philosophy of free will, or the doctrine of free will in religious circles, would have to be explored. One of the key emancipation consequences of the Socratic way of thinking was that our lives and futures weren't actually at the mercy of impersonal capricious gods; there was no actual empirical evidence that theistic forces were responsible for the triumphs or failures in our lives. We can actually determine most of what we experience in life. So what does a philosophical argument addressing the central human issue of free will look like?

This philosophical question is usually outlined as follows: *The problem of free will and determinism is this: since (1) my actions today*

---

[10] Oakely, Francis. *Community of Learning: The American College and the Liberal Arts Tradition.* New York: Oxford University Press, 1992, pp. 50-51. Print.

[11] Stanley, Thomas. *Pythagoras: His Life and Teachings.* Lake Worth: Ibis Press, 2010. Print.

[12] Hadot, Pierre. *What is Ancient Philosophy?* Translated by Michael Chase. Harvard University Press. Boston, MA, p. 55.

are determined by past events and (2) I cannot now change those past events, (3) I have no choice today as to how to act. There is a parallel argument that has an even longer history in philosophy: *(1) God knew in the past what I would do today; (2) I cannot now change what God knew in the past; therefore, (3) I have no choice today as to how to act.*

The challenge of establishing to ones and others' satisfaction whether or not our decisions or actions are entirely up to us is an ancient discussion.[13] Generally speaking, on the one hand, many have a belief that our current actions are informed by nontheistic forces stemming from a space and time in the past; on the other hand, others will choose the belief that theistic forces, existing within personal or distant dimensions, generally ordain or predestine our actions throughout our lives, free or slave. And thus, the type and level of moral responsibility we ascribe to ourselves for our actions in the world tends to be different and usually complicated by secular law.

As such, in this section, I will argue, first, that the *parallel argument* (a theistic position), while culturally acceptable within Judeo, Christian, and Islamic traditions, is a much weaker position to operate under within a secular and science-based society that must consider all members' natures of reality, including nonbelievers, and, second, while the *standard argument* presents a nontheistic position, I will argue that it represents the stronger argument but that it too has particular limits as it relates to requiring discernible casual links between current actions and past events. We begin by defining philosophically what we mean by *free will* and *determinism* in order to inform the foundational line of thought in this paper.

According to the Stanford Encyclopedia of Philosophy, free will "is a philosophical term of art for a particular sort of capacity of rational agents to choose a course of action from among various

---

[13] Kane, Robert. Free Will: Ancient Dispute, New Themes. In *Reason and Responsibility: Readings in Some Basic Problems in Philosophy, 14th ed.* Eds. Joel Fienberg and Russ Shafer-Landau. New York: Wadsworth Publishing, 2013, p. 438. Print.

alternatives."[14] The concept of free will is characterized by Kane as being one of two things: surface freedoms and/or deeper freedoms. Surface freedoms are experienced when an individual "can do whatever they want, or choose because they have been behaviorally conditioned since childhood to want and choose only what they can have and do" (p. 439). Deeper freedoms are those that are *not* "created by their behavioral conditioners and controllers."[15] Kane seems to argue that surface freedoms are informed by prior conditioning or social engineering efforts on the part of society's controllers or marketing specialists in the economic system; indeed, our controllers predetermine or manufacture what it is that we will desire, and no more than that, by what they indoctrinate, inform, or educate us with. Deeper freedoms have the least amount of prior interference from controllers in society, but since we are all born into a social, economic, and political system, we do not necessarily experience deep freedoms most of the time. As such, some of humans' locus of control is internal.

DETERMINISM

Feinberg and Shafer-Landau define *determinism* as "the theory that all events, including human actions and choices, are, without exception, totally determined."[16] For the purposes of greater specificity, I will restate the aforementioned statement on determinism as actions that are committed "today are determined

---

[14]   O'Connor, Timothy, "Free Will", *The Stanford Encyclopedia of Philosophy (Summer 2011 Edition)*, Edward N. Zalta (ed.), URL = <http://plato. stanford.edu/archives/sum2011/entries/freewill/>.

[15]   Kane, Robert. Free Will: Ancient Dispute, New Themes. In *Reason and Responsibility: Readings in Some Basic Problems in Philosophy, 14th ed.* Eds. Joel Fienberg and Russ Shafer-Landau. New York: Wadsworth Publishing, 2013, p. 439. Print.

[16]   Feinberg, Joel and Shafer-Landau, Russ. *Reason and Responsibility: Readings in Some Basic Problems in Philosophy, 14th ed.* New York: Wadsworth Publishing, 2013. Print.

by past events and (2) I cannot now change those past events, (3) I have no choice today as to how to act."[17] Conversely, indeterminism simply represents the idea that, for instance, a woman's autonomous actions may have a credible influence on how she experiences life today and tomorrow. Be that as it may, Feinberg, Shafer-Landau, and Barker describe determinism in such a way to convey that humans' choices or actions are entirely determined, or predestined, by foregoing events beyond their control. In Feinberg et al.'s description of determinism, humans can do nothing to alter their destinies in the present moment or in the future; therefore, humans' locus of control is completely external.

The other idea to explore is compatibilism; in this construct, we can have both free will and be morally responsible for our actions even if we accept that determinism is true. Feinberg and Shafer-Landau further write:

> The key issue that divides compatibilists from their opponents is usually the problem of how we should interpret "free to do otherwise," "could have done otherwise," "his act was unavoidable," and similar phrases used in support of our ascriptions of blame and punishment, credit or reward. Most parties to the discussion agree that a person can be held morally responsible for his past action *only if* he was able to do other than he did. Put more tersely: Avoidability is a necessary condition for responsibility.[18]

So it seems that a free agent also must have more than one option to choose from in order for him or her to make a free-will decision and especially to be held morally responsible for

---

[17] Barker, John. *Lecture 10 Notes on Free Will, Determinism, and Moral Responsibility.* University of Illinois-Springfield, Nov 2012. Web. 1. Nov 2012.

[18] Feinberg, Joel and Shafer-Landau, Russ. *Reason and Responsibility: Readings in Some Basic Problems in Philosophy,* 14th ed. New York: Wadsworth Publishing, 2013. p. 418. Print.

the consequences of an actual choice. This gets complicated when we insert the idea of a creator God that is responsible for predetermining our actions or our destinies.

PARALLEL ARGUMENT

Those that subscribe to the parallel argument cite Christian New Testament passages such as "in Him we have obtained an inheritance, being *predestined* according to the purpose of Him who works *all things* according to the counsel of *His will*" (Ephesians 1:11) *(emphasis mine)*.[19] In the Hebrew Bible, we read, "You saw me before I was born. Every day of my life was recorded in your book. Every moment *was laid out before* a single day passed. (Psalms 139:16)[20] Indeed, within Islamic religious sources like the Qadar, we find allusions to the idea that nothing happens unless Allah has already decreed it.[21]

As such, we see a similar line of belief amongst monotheistic religions about a form of determinism wherein it is not our free will that determines our actions and the subsequent consequences but an all-knowing, more perfect creator being existing somewhere in the external world. Unfortunately, many adherents to these belief systems tend to shift most of their moral responsibility about their actions to their "god" as well.

ARGUMENT

As I state above, the parallel argument, or the theistic position, while culturally acceptable within religious traditions like Judaism,

---

[19] *New King James Version Bible.* Nashville: Thomas Nelson Publishers, 2014. Print.

[20] *New Living Translation Bible.* Carol Stream: Tyndale House Publishers, 2007. Print.

[21] *The Hans Wehr Dictionary of Modern Written Arabic.* Ed. J.M. Cowan. Ithaca: Spoken Language Service, 1976. Print.

Christianity, and Islam, is the much weaker position to advance within a secular and science-based society that must benefit all members, including polytheists, agnostics, and nonbelievers. Correctly understood, the realm of theistic religion exists to address nonscientific life issues such as values, the relationship between man and a creator, love for mankind, and a certain way of life; in particular, an element of "faith," or as I describe it in this section *a purposeful confidence*, must be applied in conjunction with one's religious belief systems that inform our life choices or actions. Indeed, the believer has faith, or confidence, that his future will only be different or better when he or she applies the religious teachings of others, whether mono- or polytheistic based. However, the idea that God "knew" in the past what we would do today is difficult to corroborate; hence, the basis for decisions based on faith-based determinism are not rooted in evidence but quite often a consequence of capricious, arbitrary, and wishful thinking and feeling.

Faith can be problematic for many individuals depending on what sociological context they were born in. For instance, it may be problematic for an adherent of Confucian ethics, Buddhism, Hinduism, or animists, agnostics, and atheists to freely accept that, actually, a personal or impersonal God has already programmed his or her life choices. Christian teachings suggest that if a Christian has faith in God, the latter has already ordained the best course of action for the former's current and future life; subsequently through free will, she simply makes choices and actions that seem in her obvious best interest. But could religious teachings not be about pure revealed theistic-based determinism but actually be the tools of behavioral engineers that Aldous Huxley wrote about?

SURFACE FREEDOMS AND BEHAVIORAL ENGINEERS

Kane posits that we may believe we have control over some choices but that we are actually being manipulated by "advertising, television, public relations, spin doctors, salespersons, marketers, and sometimes even friends,"[22] and I would add religious and spiritual institutions. In fact, Kane's references to Aldous Huxley's *Brave New World* and B.F. Skinner's *Walden Two* seem to apply here. The residents of these fictional societies "can have and do what they will or choose, but only to the extent that they have been conditioned by behavioral engineers or neuro-chemists . . ."[23] Kane writes:

> We would be free to act or choose as we will, but would not have the ultimate say about what it is that we will. Someone else would be pulling the strings, not by coercing us against our wishes, but by manipulating us into having the wishes they wanted us to have.[24]

So it seems that while the state and marketplace are operating from a *secular realm* of influence, we can say that religious institutions may be operating from a supposed *sacred realm* of influence. Simply stated, religious teachings that suggest that a creator God has determined all of our actions beforehand are actually a different form of spiritual manipulation and serve as part of a tangible link of causation on our decisions—comforting to many, but not corroborable in the scientific sense.

[22] Kane, Robert. Free Will: Ancient Dispute, New Themes. In *Reason and Responsibility: Readings in Some Basic Problems in Philosophy, 14th ed.* Eds. Joel Fienberg and Russ Shafer-Landau. New York: Wadsworth Publishing, 2013, p. 437-8. Print.
[23] Kane, Robert. Free Will: Ancient Dispute, New Themes. In *Reason and Responsibility: Readings in Some Basic Problems in Philosophy, 14th ed.* Eds. Joel Fienberg and Russ Shafer-Landau. New York: Wadsworth Publishing, 2013, p. 438. Print.
[24] Kane, Robert. Free Will: Ancient Dispute, New Themes. In *Reason and Responsibility: Readings in Some Basic Problems in Philosophy, 14th ed.* Eds. Joel Fienberg and Russ Shafer-Landau. New York: Wadsworth Publishing, 2013, p. 438. Print.

THE STANDARD ARGUMENT

The standard argument, which I have established as the nontheistic position, has wider applicability in the lives of most human beings of the developing and developed worlds; and this is because it is more difficult to prove the parallel argument, or begin to provide basic objective evidence, for a direct causal influence of a specific intangible deity on our decision-making processes.

As cited above, the standard arguments says that "since (1) my actions today are determined by past events, and (2) I cannot now change those past events, (3) I have no choice today as to how to act." In the natural realm, it seems more possible to make at least weak connections to, or corroborate associations between, past events and some of our present decisions.

Barker uses Tourette's syndrome symptoms to highlight an example of the standard argument; he accomplishes this by differentiating the differences between what seems to be an act without free will (Tourette's syndrome symptoms) and one that seems also to have causal links to establish the point that we all, potentially, experience a chain of deterministic causation about our actions. He writes:

> Intuitively, the difference is that the Tourette's victim's outburst is caused by something over which he has no control: in this case, some abnormal feature of his brain chemistry. But is this actually any different from your own case? Your action is caused by some brain state of yours. Do you really have control over this brain state? Well, maybe you think that you do control this. However, your outburst was, in fact, only the final link in a very long causal chain C1, . . . Cn, with Cn being the outburst itself. Cn has some cause Cn1, which is some state of your brain prior to your outburst. But Cn1 itself is caused by some preceding state Cn2 of your brain, or perhaps of your

brain-plus-body-plus-environment. Pushing this causal chain further and further back, we see that the whole chain is actually caused by some state of the universe at some time in the remote past. And surely that is outside your control.[25]

It seems that whether we think we act with surface or deep freedoms, there can be a level of discernment about a causal chain of events which inform our current actions. Thus, standard arguments, by using empirically based results from brain research on Tourette's syndrome, have greater legitimacy and a stronger position when understanding determinism; a religiously based parallel argument attempting to explain the roots of Tourette's syndrome would usually posit the idea that evil spirits or the victim's parents were somehow morally, not genetically, responsible for a Tourette's syndrome victim's outbursts. Barker further argues that generally speaking:

> Human action is a (basically) rational process. You store information about the world, derived primarily from your sense organs: this is called belief. You also have certain preferences or desires: certain states that you try to get into, or states of the world that you try to bring about. And for the most part, you act in the way that is most likely to satisfy your preferences, at least relative to your beliefs. A compatibilist might hold that a free action is one that is produced in the normal way by one's beliefs and desires.

It seems then that a level of free will finds an association with our stored information that came into our senses from many different sources, and we often choose to categorize them as

---

[25]   Professor John Barker. Lecture 10 Notes on Free will, Determinism, and Moral Responsibility. University of Illinois-Springfield, 2012. Web. 1 Nov 2013.

knowledge or beliefs; these sources of information can be religious teachings, secular education, or knowledge sharing in the social context. But are all beliefs bad for humans and are all humans' actions basically rational processes?

OBJECTIONS

While there may be continuing disagreement about whether or not a belief based on religious faith can be counted as knowledge, a belief that a creator God predestined all or most of our actions is not illegal or harmful if experienced appropriately; such beliefs that cannot be empirically corroborated simply should not, in turn, be used to inform public policy or marketplace strategies as these potentially affect nonbelievers in society. Faith in a creator God should remain a private matter for free and nonfree human beings; many religious beliefs can bring private comfort and reconciliation between neighbors. Indeed, this must also hold true for standard arguments that cannot establish a direct causal link between past events and potential current and future decisions.

Second, while it may be true that most human actions are basically rational, this may not be true in all global societies. Moreover, while it is true that feelings are intangible and not always rooted in reason, they are nonetheless real at some level for human beings. Yes, in our current age, supposed truth claims must be empirically verified in a credible way in order for them to inform courses of action that will impact animals, human lives, and natural resources. Again, Yale University professor of medicine Steven Novella posits that, at a basic level, natural effects like Tourette's syndrome symptoms must be explained as having natural causes and not rooted in a category of the miraculous, supernatural, or, I might add, the spiritual.

FINDINGS

Can free will and some level of determinism coexist without much controversy? I believe they can. When we understand that prior actions have current consequences, there does seem to be enough rationale for accepting that discernible forgoing actions may have good or bad effects now and in the future. It seems to me that problems begin to arise when certain parties attempt to make social or public policy based *only* on theistic-based or indiscernible determinism constructs; again, these are difficult to discern and corroborate as evidence that may impact the lives of others, free or otherwise.

Eventually, the enterprise of secular philosophy would encounter a stiff challenge from Christian theology as a way to deal with humans' fear of imminent death or simply to understand life on Earth better.[26] Philosophy would maintain its legitimacy for many centuries, at least as the handmaiden of theology, until it regained its rightful autonomy during the modern era; it would also be classified with greater specificity, especially as Western civilization moved into the postmodern era. This greater specificity would produce broader understanding through an early form of interdisciplinary curricula.

Philosophy: interdisciplinary for broad learning

Philosophical understanding and dialogue tends also to take on the nature of an interdisciplinary search for truth; it is not necessarily a discussion among only one type of specialist but between different and related specialists or disciplines. Using this approach develops a broader habit of mind. According to twentieth century historian Will Durant, philosophy includes

---

[26]   Ferry, Luc. *A Brief History of Thought: A Philosophical Guide to Living.* New York: Harper-Perennial, 2003. Print.

five disciplinary fields: logic, ethics, politics, esthetics, and metaphysics.[27] Thus, it seems that, for Durant, *philosophy* addresses issues of right reasoning, what actions we ought to engage in to produce better outcomes for others and ourselves, the exercise of political institutions and influence, what may be considered beautiful or tasteful in the world, and what is the nature of reality.

For instance, if pharmacy students are discussing the challenges and opportunities involved in the use of a new medicine or drug, the educational process should involve questions that (1) produce a clearer understanding of the medicine's design and purpose, (2) require the full disclosure of its proper use and risks, (3) clarify what regulatory agencies or legislative agendas must be considered, (4) establish initial recommendations about the medicine's access or packaging in the marketplace, and (5) inform students how the general public or various religious groups may react to the medicine in question. Thus, we see the potential for a broader understanding of the complexities involved with new medicine introduction, marketing, and its proper use. These discussions involve not only the facts of scientific discovery but also the values that philosophy brings to improve medicine and its applications.

At the outset of the twenty-first century, author and philosopher Stephen Law posits that there are generally seven branches of the philosophy tree. These seven branches include *epistemology*, the study of knowledge or how we know what we know, and which addresses the issue of skepticism and the differences between reason and experience; *metaphysics*, which attempts to address the fundamental issues of ontology or the nature of reality in the world; *moral philosophy*, wherein the topic of ethics and what we should do are explored; the *philosophy of mind*, which attempts to answer the question of what the mind is as the essence of human thought; *the philosophy of evil*, which explores the problem of evil, faith, reason, and whether or not God

---

[27]   Durant, Will. *The Story of Philosophy: The Lives and Opinions of the Great Philosopher*. New York: Simon & Schuster, 1943, p. 3. Print.

exists; *political philosophy*, that examines how the common good may be characterized and in the context of the liberal political ideal; and finally, one of the oldest, the *philosophy of science*, wherein the use of inductive reason, the scientific method, and the need for falsification of current scientific theory is necessary for its continuing legitimacy.[28]

Thus, the enterprise of philosophy as an educational process tool addresses multidimensional aspects of the human experience at the individual and social levels. Philosophy not only addresses multidimensional aspects of life, but it most importantly infuses the dialogue about life with questions about what values should inform the proper use of new discoveries, our relationships with others, and how we think through and solve our dilemmas. Invariably, if the objective of philosophy is to discern between truth and falsehood or the rightness or wrongness of an action, then invariably the issue of what values should inform these questions comes into the dialogue.

PHILOSOPHY AND PERSONAL DEVELOPMENT

And so, what draws many to philosophically informed questions that address the need to better understand ourselves, others, and our natural world, regardless of race, culture, or language group, is that they address an inner desire for not simply more wisdom but also what Rousseau called *perfectibility*, that is the ability to improve ourselves throughout life to become a better human being and ideally for others. Indeed, according to Rousseau, the desire to improve ourselves is what separates us from nonhuman creatures who tend to exhibit predetermined, or "programmed," natures generally; it is the human being who exercises reasoned free will when making self-interested and disinterested decisions intended for personal

---

[28]   Law, Stephen. *Visual Reference Guide, Philosophy*. New York: Metro Books, 2012. Print.

advantage to change and improve ourselves, others, or the realities in the world at large.

The idea of philosophy as the search for truth, a way of life, or the love of wisdom seems simple enough to understand but also often conditional to time, place, and culture. However, in virtually all cases, it seems that accepted wisdom contains not only timeless value but also *values* that enlighten ways of living the world over, not simply temporary and valuable insights about a current situation. Usually, whether it's Socrates or the ideas and questions posed by other revered historical figures like Buddha, Confucius, Christ, Averroes, or Martin Luther King, lives are changed in positive and sometimes in painful ways.

Oftentimes, very wise individuals utter very unpopular ideas, indeed threatening, to the status quo or even the powerless, inducing hate and not love about the speaker's supposed wise words. For instance, Socrates argued that knowledge was synonymous with virtue as knowing more about what is just increases the possibility that we ourselves could apply more justice to our dealings with others, and this sometimes meant doing some good toward our enemies. This argument about the truly just person challenged the prevailing common sense in Athenian society and differentiated between ideas about what *was* occurring and what *ought* to occur. But knowing right and doing good deeds can be two different things.

Oftentimes, knowing what the wise thing to do is not enough to produce just actions among human beings as most important dilemmas are complicated and contain too many known and unknown variables to consider; prevailing political environments and personal preferences or prejudices often cloud the efforts of what should be the most *just* decision for a given situation. Thus, it is reasonable to apply a healthy skepticism to what educational, religious, or political leaders say or document as they are fallible human beings. More often than not, it is the virtue of *courage* that is in short supply, and this seems understandable as when humans face difficult dilemmas or new situations. And so, it seems the intelligent emotion of informed courage can serve a positive purpose by propelling us forward in applying knowledge to many of life's opportunities or difficult challenges. But is important knowledge necessarily the same thing as wisdom?

As mentioned earlier, wisdom should have a timeless value, but many times, what we currently *know* very often becomes outdated, serving no further purpose in the search for truth or a better way of life. But can a fragment of current knowledge graduate to the level of lasting wisdom? Management guru Peter Drucker argued that information is, basically, data infused with *relevance* and *purpose*. Perhaps the same idea can be applied to the conceptual stages connecting knowledge and wisdom; that is, for the former to qualify as the latter, it should be not only relevant to a current situation but also serve to inform higher purposes in our world. This can include our personal lives or the organization we work for.

In the case of an organizational crisis, the information contained in a reliable knowledge management system, perhaps input from a consultant or the results of a group brainstorming process, can produce greater clarity that informs a better course of action that fulfills the current organizational mission and this while sustaining the organization's long-term vision and values about serving customers with ethical principles. However, within the current era of globalization, which invariably involves cross-cultural exchanges and the inevitable interpersonal misunderstandings, managers and employees are often unaware that what is considered unethical or illegal in one culture will be considered legal in another.

Ideally, training or professional development in global business culture, or in specific cross-cultural competencies, can help and organization's members better understand key cultural differences and, just as important, universal human values (see Chapter 4, Table 2). Thus, it becomes more possible to accomplish organizational and/or social goals with potentially fewer mistakes. Indeed, in the current era of globalization, engaging in international trade, diplomacy, or travel is most especially an opportunity to discover and develop these common universal values.

Perennial philosophies, herein understood to represent lasting universal human values about the nature of reality which transcend culture, time, and place, can serve as the dialogical vehicles that connect us to a wider professional and cultural world community; we can, therefore, discover more human commonality than dissimilarity. This commonality is not necessarily predetermined uniformity per se but a sense of psychological, professional, and spiritual affinity with others in our common attempts to achieve more clarity about our lives, our work, and indeed the human experience on Earth. Learning to appreciate more about the *other* has the potential for increasing respect for what is different and interesting between diverse peoples, languages, customs, and cultures; oftentimes, however, this is not necessarily a guarantee if learning about or experiencing others also is not rooted in the solving of common human challenges and opportunities.

Dialogical experiences, therefore, about perennial philosophies is one educational approach which attempts to create and sustain, without arriving at final answers, deeper discussions not only about how best to conduct our lives but also about how better to begin to understand the experience of others, near and far; thus, we initiate and develop further a cross-cultural habit of mind, especially when encountering social contexts dominated by members of the "other."

Indeed, it is mainly through the philosophically rooted education and learning enterprise wherein we experience the intentional initiation and development of a deeper and broader mindset, which is so evident throughout, for example, the dialogues of Plato's *Republic,* arguably an early form of liberal education and learning. As we will see in subsequent chapters, Socrates, Plato, Aristotle, and other historical figures such as Hypatia, the only woman who taught philosophy and mathematics at the Library of Alexandria, would establish themselves as the first liberal arts professorate as they would dialogue and create lasting change about many important human issues pertaining to justice, courage, virtue, ethics, science, and many others that still inform our contemporary world. Thus, we now turn to a more concrete discussion about the background and value of a liberal education for the twenty-first century.

CHAPTER 2

LIBERAL EDUCATION: A CHECKERED HISTORY

But there is only one real liberal study, that which
gives a man his liberty. It is the study of wisdom,
and that is lofty, brave, and great-souled.

Seneca (4 B.C.E.—A.D. 65)

🦉 🦉 🦉

Arguably, the first revolution in higher learning, herein synonymous with liberal learning, among humans occurred in the streets of Athens during the latter part of the fifth century BCE; this was where Socrates initiated his critical thinking project as the ever famous gadfly of Athens. As a consequence, there was a definite paradigm shift, or change, in the way many free Athenians thought and felt about their attitudes, values, and beliefs; this shift would eventually engulf much of Western civilization, indeed, largely as a result of early but vibrant liberal education institutions.

GREEK INITIATION

As recounted in Plato's *Republic*, Socrates's way of living began to encourage many in Athens to climb out of the cave of intellectual darkness and cultural illusions and into the light of better understanding. Many Athenians could afford to benefit from this new kind of intellectual and spiritual freedom, but others could not; many who chose not to understood very clearly that playing the fool in the depths of the cave offered particular economic and social membership benefits in the Grecian cosmos. Certainly, there is comfort in familiar and established customs and especially for those like Socrates's wealthy friend Cephalus who, we understand from *Republic*'s Book I, was at the end of his life and presumably felt comfortable with the status quo; however, the seeds of change and revolution are often planted among the idealistic young, and they would be in Cephalus's son Polemarchus and others. Cephalus was not interested in dialoguing with Socrates at a deeper level about what was just or not in Athenian society. However, within this same encounter, Thrasymachus, a sophist representing the threatened old guard, aggressively challenges the very idea that Socrates is attempting to put forward, specifically, an idea that would redefine the established concept of justice in Athens that was based only on raw power or political privilege.

In addition to the abuse of political privilege, it seemed to become increasingly evident to Socrates that biases and bigotry based on superstition, religious agendas, racial mythologies, or defective nationalism threaten to retard human development and, by extension, civilization. By initiating unsanctioned and controversial dialogue about justice, friendship, piety, war, treatment of enemies, and other sacred cows, Socrates would essentially liberate his friends and audiences to engage in real world problem solving conversations. Thus, in theory, at least a liberal education promises to *liberate* the individual from the dark caverns of intellectual and social backwardness as recounted in Plato's *Allegory of the Cave*. Without the opportunity for the free individual to uproot from his soul harmful belief frameworks, a flourishing life, or what Aristotle called *Eudemonia,* will be less likely for him or society as a whole. Thus was the age of education, characterized by a genuine search for truth among the people at the street level, begun through dialogue about justice and privilege;

forms of indoctrination would remain, but a new way to establish new understanding was briskly under way.

Subsequent to the fifth century BCE, many Athenians no longer behaved as dependent children to be fed by higher authorities what to think, feel, or believe about their complicated lives. Essentially, Socrates had begun the process of human emancipation by initiating an early form of liberal education method involving dialogue and critical thinking; this would equip the individual in knowing *how* to think, not simply *what* to think, about many of life's complicated issues. But this would deeply concern the religious and political elites in Athens who maintained intellectual, spiritual, and cultural control over the lives of free Athenians by demanding unthinking allegiance to Greek gods and customs.

Be that as it may, we find in Plato's *Republic* book six the early semblances of the liberal arts curricula. Philosophy is established as the foundation of education in society, in fact, "if philosophy ever finds in the State that perfection which she herself is, then will be seen that she is in truth divine" (205). Later in book six, the dialogue turns its attention to intellectual or educational categories. Plato writes:

> Next proceed to consider the manner in which the sphere of the intellectual is to be divided . . . Thus: There are two divisions . . . You are aware that students of geometry, arithmetic, and the kindred sciences assume the odd, and the even, and the figures, and the three kinds of angles, and the like, in their several branches of science (221).[29]

Above, we begin to discern the first of the two major academic divisions we know as the quadrivium that eventually came to include the disciplines of mathematics, music, geometry, and

---

[29]   Plato. *Republic.* Translated by Benjamin Jewett. New York, NY: Barnes & Noble Classics, 2004, p. 221. Print.

astronomy. Plato would also outline the second of the major academic divisions; he writes:

> And when I speak of the other division of the intelligible, you will understand me to speak of that other sort of knowledge which reason itself attains by the power of dialectic, using the hypotheses not as first principles, but only as hypotheses . . . (222).[30]

Here, we discern the beginnings of what would be considered the trivium, or the dialectical sciences, involving grammar, logic, and rhetoric; these three disciplines are necessary to engage in effective dialogue and deeper dialectics. Thus, the former we understand as the mathematical sciences and the latter as dialectical sciences.

Ultimately, poisoned blood would have to run through the veins of Socrates in order for his revolution in thinking, learning, and living to be sustainable. While it is safe to assume that many Athenians like Plato and subsequent generations of free peoples no longer felt it appropriate to blindly receive truth as unquestioning children, it would, in fact, take formalized institutions of higher learning, as vehicles of liberal education, which would sustain human emancipation into the future.

GRECO-ROMAN LEARNING

As outlined above, the origins of the liberal arts tradition began in the eastern Mediterranean and stemming mainly from Plato's dialogues; these powerful dialogues included the heavy participation of his teacher Socrates and the early manifestations of critical inquiry, rhetoric, and dialectical forms of discussion centered on key questions. The core liberal arts curricula, henceforth synonymous with the term *liberal learning*, represent

---

[30]   Ibid.

the conceptual contraction of what in Plato's *Republic* are called the dialectical sciences and the mathematical sciences; these two major categories would be organized in a later era as both the *trivium* and the *quadrivium,* respectively.

The trivium curricula would be comprised of courses in grammar, logic, and rhetoric, and the quadrivium would be composed of courses in mathematics, music, geometry, and astronomy; both major curricular sections would ultimately be coalesced during the medieval era into the Seven Liberal Arts (circa twelfth Century). Indeed, the Seven Liberal Arts seem to provide for balanced interdisciplinary regimens of higher learning involving, for example, the arts and sciences (grammar and astronomy), the development of theory to inform practice (mathematics and music), and the linear concepts that complement new visual communications in very nonlinear ways (geometry and rhetoric).

Author H.L. Haywood provides a poetic description from a seventeenth century publication entitled the *Ahiman Rezon* about the particular purposes and personal impact that the liberal arts curricula can have on a learner:

> The grammar rules instruct the tongue and pen, Rhetoric teaches eloquence to men; By logic we are taught to reason well, Music has claims beyond our power to tell; The use of numbers, numberless we find; Geometry gives measure to mankind. The heavenly system elevates the mind.[31]

The forgoing poetic example of the purpose and specific influences of the liberal arts on an individual's actual or potential capabilities speaks to the power of an intentional curricular design intended to develop further a human being's cognitive, psychomotor, and spiritual dimensions. Liberal education impinges

---

[31]   Haywood, H.L. *The Masonic Liberal Arts and Sciences.* Whitefish: Kessinger Publishing, 2010, p. 236. Print.

upon the individual's soul from external sources to, subsequently, enable him or her to understand better and articulate how they see and can improve the world around them.

While Haywood may use the sequence of grammar, rhetoric, and logic to explain the trivium above, others prefer to use a different sequence for the trivium such as grammar, logic, and rhetoric; indeed, I argue that an effective communicator must first know basic language structures (grammar) and develop critical reasoning competencies (logic) to understand and evaluate her information better in order to subsequently use effective persuasion approaches (rhetoric) with an individual or audience.

Often confused with a connotation denoting the opposite of political *conservatism*, *liberal* education during the Greek and Roman eras was understood to be a form of higher learning fit for the free citizen and, I would add by extension, the form of education that sustains and evolves the institutions of a free society. Indeed, by engaging in a liberal arts curriculum designed to foster appreciation for history, what is different, healthy skepticism about new information, and cognitive dissonance about the many assumptions we apply to understand others, the individual initiates and sustains intellectual and social membership within the larger human and technical community. One of Socrates's students, Plato, believed in a liberal learning environment that attempted to engender a love of wisdom within future political leaders.

PLATO'S ACADEMY

Much different from his teacher Socrates who dialogued in the streets, Plato would establish his academy in Athens in a physical building and actually establish prerequisites in geometry before matriculation could be achieved into his school. Plato's Academy offered varied curricula, but its chief curriculum was designed to educate men and women in advanced levels of political philosophy. One of Plato's chief works, the *Republic,* addresses many aspects of Athenian life, and its first dialogue would explore what could characterize the just *polis* or political community during their era. But his ideas of the just society, comprising generally three ranks of citizens, namely the merchants, the warrior class, and the philosopher kings, have been characterized as elitist or, at worst, authoritarian. Plato was not fond of democratic forms of society or governance as it was Athenian democracy that sentenced his teacher Socrates to death in 399 BCE.

Nonetheless, Plato believed that if kings, or political leaders, were educated in philosophy, essentially becoming lovers of wisdom, better decisions could be made within the political community, at least for free Athenians. Hadot writes:

> The Sophists had claimed to train young people for political life, but Plato wanted to accomplish this by providing them with a knowledge far superior to that which the Sophists could give them. On the other hand, this knowledge was to be founded upon a rigorous rational method; on the other, in accordance with the Socratic concept, it was to be inseparable from the love of the good and from the inner transformation of the person. Plato wanted to train not only skillful statesmen, but also human beings.[32]

Plato desired to use reason and ethics to train statesmen that could be characterized as humanistic in nature. The Sophists, on the other hand, were experts at teaching their students how to make a weaker argument more appealing to unwitting audiences, however bad its inherent idea was, and also in inculcating their audiences with the notion that all human beliefs were essentially relative; according to the Sophists, many ideas are not better or worse—they're just simply different.

The Sophists' approach would seem to weaken a society and set its citizens on a perilous course according to some ancient and

---

[32] Hadot, Pierre. *What is ancient philosophy?* Translated by Michael Chase. Harvard University Press. Boston, MA, 2004, p. 59.

Modern era philosophers. For example, W. K. Clifford (1845-1879) warns against operating under weak or unjustified beliefs, stating that we "all suffer enough from the maintenance and support of false beliefs and the fatally wrong actions which they lead to, and the evil born when one such belief is entertained great and wide."[33] This dangerous consequence also can occur within dogmatic and sectarian communities wherein a religious or political entity's ideological stances are given the status of absolute truths; the necessary dissent required for a healthy critique of beliefs in the world are instead discouraged, if not outlawed, by leaders or the state. Would that many Germans, Italians, or Spaniards during the early part of the twentieth century in Europe questioned early enough the ideas of Hitler, Mussolini, and Franco and not given in to the seeming stability that fascism promised but rarely delivers.

Plato's ideas of the ideal political community were actually meant to be experienced first within his learning community at the academy; he believed that if the ideals and goals for free and equal citizenship could not first be experienced within the educational context, then operationalizing them within the city would be less possible. Thus, key elements of the Platonic liberal curriculum included a commitment to reason and egalitarian dialogue experienced within a residential environment. One of the Academy's longstanding students, Aristotle, would extend new ways of thinking by pioneering, in particular, an early form of scientific inquiry (empiricism) by examining and cataloguing various findings from the world of ideas, experience, and nature.

ARISTOTLE'S LYCEUM

While Plato's Academy would represent a liberal curriculum centered on ideas and theory, Aristotle's Lyceum represented a

---

[33]   Clifford, W.K. Reason and Faith: The Ethics of Belief. In *Reason and Responsibility: Readings in Some Basic Problems in Philosophy,* 14th Ed. Eds. Joel Feinberg and Russ Shafer-Landau. New York: Wadsworth Publishing p. 120. Print.

different way of searching for truth in the world of liberal learning; Aristotle differed with his teacher Plato about what constituted reality or truth. The former believed that truth could only be ascertained through direct experience within the world of matter around us; he believed in tangible realities, not constructs that resided only in the invisible minds of humans. The curriculum offered through the Lyceum concentrated on concrete subjects like ethics, logic, biology, botany, private property, and others. Interestingly, while Plato believed in educating both men and women as equals, Aristotle thought that women were essentially defective males. In 343 BCE, King Philip of Macedon would establish the Mieza School and place Aristotle as its headmaster; his most famous student would be King Philip's son, Alexander the Great, who would remain Aristotle's protégé the rest of his life. Alexander would die at the age of thirty-three with the blood-filled hands of an unfulfilled conqueror. Hellenistic Greek culture began its gradual decline and would end roughly in 31 BCE at the Battle of Actium with the emergent Romans.

Nonetheless, Greek thought, philosophies, and teachers would inform and serve as a key source of knowledge for the emerging Roman Empire during the first century BCE. While most Roman children were educated by their fathers at home,[34] the majority of the elite's children were taught by Greek teachers liberal studies such as philosophy, rhetoric, grammar, and other academic areas fit for those being groomed for future leadership roles in the empire. While the Greeks specialized in the development of intangible ideas, philosophy, and theory, the Romans were primarily interested in applying practical knowledge; this would enable the latter to build networks of roads throughout its vast empire, specialize in architecture, exploit engineering theory for building bridges and water aqueducts, develop republican government and the legal system to underpin it, and deploy a military machine that could support and sustain the political goals of the Roman senate. In

---

[34]   Lucas, Christopher J. *American Higher Education: A History*. New York: St, Martins Griffin, 1994. Print.

northern Egypt, the world's earliest knowledge management system existed at the Library of Alexandria wherein most of the world's knowledge about science, philosophy, engineering, war, religion, culture, and many languages were archived. The most famous of the library's teachers and philosophers was Hypatia (circa AD 351-450) who taught astronomy and philosophy there.

HYPATIA

Across the Mediterranean Sea from Rome lived and taught Hypatia, a Greek Neo-Platonist philosopher who would specialize in ethics, mathematics, metaphysics, and astronomy. She was her father's closest collaborator in his work involving philosophy, mathematics, and esoteric subjects. She also would be considered Alexandria's favorite philosopher among Christians, Jews, and pagans alike.[35]

While there are few remains of her work, there are letters written by some of her students that shed light on what she was known for. In a letter written by Synesius of Cyrene to his best friend, Herculian, who would become a prefect in Constantinople, the former expresses delight about the educational experience they had both received from Hypatia, describing it as "a voyage in which it was granted to you and me to experience marvelous things, the bare recital of which had seemed to us incredible! We have seen with our eyes, we have heard with our ears the lady who legitimately presided over the mysteries of philosophy."[36]

Unfortunately, her chaste life would be violently ended by a corrupt and power hungry Christian patriarch named Cyril. Cyril would succeed his uncle Theophilus in AD 412 through bloody

---

[35] Rubenstein, Richard E. *Aristotle's Children, How Christians, Muslims, and Jews Rediscovered Ancient Wisdom and Illuminated the Middle Ages.* San Diego, CA: A Harvest Book Harcourt, Inc., 2004, pp. 68-69.

[36] Pollard, Justin and Reid, Howard. *The Rise and Fall of Alexandria Birthplace of the Modern World.* New York, NY: Penguin Books, 2007, p. 268. Print.

and violent battles in the streets of Alexandria. Not content to be a part of the largest religious group in this city, Cyril inspired and led many pogroms against one of Alexandria's oldest community the Jews. His allies, the Nitrian monks who resided in the desert, were inspired by Cyril to attack who they saw as the chief pagan Hypatia so as to purify the land for their religious sect. In the end, Hypatia would be murdered by these priests in a church, but after his death, Cyril would, subsequently, be declared a saint and a doctor of the Christian church.[37]

However, with increasing internal moral decay, political corruption, and ongoing civil wars throughout the empire, Rome became increasingly vulnerable to the barbarians at the periphery of the empire and fell into absolute decline. After centuries of marked progress, Greco-Roman and Western civilization at large experienced a reversal of real progress and fortunes, ultimately collapsing politically in the late fifth century AD.

Lights out for the West

For roughly a thousand years in the wake of the demise of Roman civilization (circa AD 476), life in the Christian West existed mainly in intellectual darkness, religious superstition, diseased-proned environments, and economic poverty. According to H.L. Haywood, scholars in Europe during "the so called Dark Ages . . . devoted themselves almost entirely to studies that had little or no connection with human life; they debated such questions as, What are the attributes of Deity? What are angels? What are demons? . . . How many angels can stand on the point of a needle?"[38] However, within Islamic civilization, a different intellectual and social environment was emerging.

[37] Pollard, Justin and Reid, Howard. *The Rise and Fall of Alexandria Birthplace of the Modern World.* New York, NY: Penguin Books, 2007, pp. 272-279. Print.

[38] Haywood, H.L. *The Masonic Liberal Arts and Sciences*, Whitefish: Kessinger Publishing, 2010, p. 237.

While scholarship and research had always been a part of Islamic civilization, the Golden Age of Islam began in the eighth century AD, and it would be scholars and scientists from throughout the Arab and Persian worlds that would create, shepherd, and extend knowledge in science, literature, medicine, algebra, and philosophy for roughly two centuries. For instance, *Ibn al-Haythum* (AD 965-AD 1040) of Basra, Iraq, considered a key place for the beginning of learning, would later refine and publish books on, among other subjects, the "scientific method" and disseminate his findings in as faraway places at medieval Spain.

Indeed, one of the key early sources of the Western rebirth occurred during the twelfth century through the infusion into Andalusian Spain of Arab thought and scholarship, which had itself been informed by Indian, Persian, and Grecian ideas. It would be in this region of southwestern Europe wherein Iberian Jewish and Christian scholars would be initiated by Arab scholars into Aristotelian ideas and their potential application to medieval life.[39] This important collaboration had been made possible in southern Spain as the three major theistic Abrahamic faiths were committed during this time to cross-cultural tolerance and mutual inquiry.

In addition to Grecian ideas, Islamic doctors of medicine would infuse Galen's work on medicinal praxis, and their own extensions of medical knowledge, back into Italy. According to Eugen Weber, professor of history at the University of California Los Angeles, the entire teaching staff at the opening of the medical school at Salerno in Italy was of Islamic origins. The study of law could be pursued at the University of Bologna in Italy and the queen of the sciences, theology, at the University of Paris in France; during this time, philosophy would serve as the handmaiden of theology as the powers of philosophical reasoning would be used to affirm what the Church considered to be its higher revealed truths.

---

[39] Rubenstein, Richard E. *Aristotle's Children, How Christians, Muslims, and Jews Rediscovered Ancient Wisdom and Illuminated the Middle Ages.* San Diego, CA: A Harvest Book Harcourt, Inc., 2004. Print.

In the sacred architectural realm, Brunelleschi in Italy, under the patronage of the Medici dynasty, would also reach back into Roman antiquity to better understand the classical architectural arts and sciences to complete the *Dome of the Basilica di Santa Maria del Fiore*; henceforth, Florence, Italy would enter into the early stages of a European era that celebrated and developed further the human spirit and mind. Moreover, with the rediscovery of Aristotle's ideas about the importance of reason and experience, the Christian church would use a reasoning tool, called apologetics, to defend its version of revealed truths and their influence on Christian theology through what became known as *Scholasticism* (circa twelfth to sixteenth centuries AD); Thomas Aquinas's most famous work entitled *Summa Theologica* was completed in the late thirteenth century and was probably the most influential Scholastics work of the period leading up to the rebirth of Western civilization, better known as the Renaissance.

THE RENAISSANCE AND THE HUMANITIES

While the work of Thomas Aquinas achieved a synthesis involving Aristotelian reason and Christian faith, the educational emphasis during the medieval era generally would remain on the Creator, Christian ethics, and the afterlife, as defined by the Catholic Church, but yet sustain an indifference to the value of human contributions to the nature of reality on earth. According to religious and political authorities in the Christian West, the individual could not be trusted and must be kept in intellectual darkness and in a state of the fear of eternal damnation.

With the advent of the Renaissance, some dominions in the Western world began to value and encourage human agency and what we call the humanities. The rediscovery of Grecian ideas on human beauty, for instance, with its primary focus on human symmetry in structure, initiated a new emphasis in how artistic work centered on various human subjects, or architectural works, could elevate the human spirit in a museum or cathedral church.

A renewed interest also in "this worldly" knowledge and thinking would be initiated and spread to other parts of medieval Europe. A rediscovery of the writings of historians, such as Herodotus, Nero, or Thucydides, among others, informed the idea that, by comparing older civilizations to present ones, human progress could be discernible and encouraged on into the future.[40] Paolo Vergerio (1370-1444) wrote that "written records are very valuable indeed for other purposes, they are especially valuable for preserving the memory of the past, as they contain the deeds of mankind, the unhoped-for turns of fortune, the unusual works of nature, and (more important than all these things) the guiding principles of historical periods."[41]

The humanities curriculum designed to educate learners about the humane arts and letters would, however, experience rejection within the clergy-dominated universities in Europe during this time as humanistic learning focused mainly on the creature and not the Creator in the cosmos. But new academies would instead be established in places like Italy to advance learning in art, poetry, literature, music, languages, and esoteric subjects like alchemy and astrology. According to Fernandez-Armesto, rediscovering the knowledge taught within the mystery schools of ancient Egypt regarding supposed magical processes involved in transforming base metal into gold would not only appeal to those interested in materialistic gain but also encourage renewed interest in alchemy, what would later become chemistry, as practiced by Isaac Newton and later Moderns.

The ancient insights of astrology would evolve in the Renaissance period into the scientific field of astronomy. In fact, Nicolaus Copernicus (AD 1473-1543) would validate astronomy through a

---

[40] Fernandez-Armesto-Felipe. *Ideas That Shaped Mankind: A Concise History of Human Thought.* Portable Professor, Recorded Books. New York: Barnes & Noble Publishing, 2005.

[41] Vergerio, Pier Paolo. Character and Studies Befitting a Free-Born Youth. In *The Great Tradition: Classic Readings on What I Means to Be an Educated Human Being.* Ed. Richard M. Gamble. Wilmington: ISI Books, 2008, p. 317. Print.

powerful idea called the *heliocentric cosmology*, which radically altered our understanding of earth's position and role within our solar system, specifically, that the Earth revolves around the sun and not the other way around. Sadly, it would be Galileo who would later pay the price of exile for this new discovery at the hands of the Inquisition in Rome that was more interested in preserving temporal power than in new *natural* revelation; Galileo, through the use of his telescope, confirmed Copernicus's theory on the heliocentric cosmology. In the end, it would be Johannes Kepler (1571-1630) who would alter Copernicus's theory and instead posit that the orbits of the planets did not revolve around the sun in a circular fashion, as Aristotle and Copernicus believed, but in an elliptical way. Increasingly, for many scientists, knowledge is to be viewed as tentative and subject to change upon the consideration of new data in a certain field.

Since the closure of the Plato's Academy by Roman emperor Justin in AD 529, philosophy had fallen into obscurity or simply served as the handmaiden of theology. However, Descartes (AD 1596-1650), the father of modern philosophy, argued for the idea that it was only through deductive reasoning (i.e., using general premises to understand specific instances), not necessarily through sense perceptions, was where reliable ways of constructing new understanding was possible. Moreover, Descartes's ideas about skepticism were important to the development of the research ideal, meaning that we must approach all phenomena without preconceived notions, biases, or prejudices but in most cases with doubt. Thus, impetus was provided by these manifold sources for rediscovery of non-Western and secular Greco-Roman ideas and knowledge. Indeed, the power and increasing influence of the humanities and natural sciences, in particular, during the Age of Reason would remain and inform the emerging Modern era.

Modernity

Through the benefit of humanistic disciplines, such as history or sociology, and the application of Socratic forms of critical thinking, free citizens are better able to learn and benefit from the past in crucial ways. Harvard University philosopher and poet George Santayana aptly warned many years ago that "those who cannot remember the past are condemned to repeat it."[42] Without the benefit of informed hindsight outlined in historical accounts about what has not worked previously in various global societies (sociology), coupled with an open but questioning mind about new messages coming from those entrusted with authority, indeed, from those who make value-laden decisions about a society's future, the necessary analysis and discernment to make reasoned judgments about leaders' statements may not occur.

The failure of citizens to critically analyze leaders' words and deeds can lead to the loss of essential hard fought political rights, new ideas, scientific discoveries, ecological protections, and social freedoms; and so, in the worst-case scenario, religious and political authoritarianism achieves seeming stability but hardly any new progress in the social, spiritual, or scientific realms as new ideas have always threatened these two ancient and entrenched power structures of society. Many American colonists would apply enlightenment thinking to their social and economic compact with mother England, revolt after finding it wanting, and achieve a level of national independence but not necessarily culturally for some time.

BACON'S NEW ATLANTIS?

In the burgeoning United States, Harvard University (1636), College of William & Mary (1693), Yale University (1701), and Princeton University (1746) were the first of the colonial colleges; these were followed by what would become the University of Pennsylvania, Columbia University, Brown University, Rutgers University, and Dartmouth College. Generally speaking, with

---

[42] Santayana, George. *Reason in Common Sense, volume 1 of The Life of Reason.* New York: Scribners, 1905, p. 284. Print.

the exception of the College of William & Mary, which offered a course in surveying, most of the colonial colleges offered a classical curriculum focused mainly on grammar, meaning the formal study in Greek, Latin, and Hebrew languages; many educators wanted to expand the curriculum, and many elites were dissatisfied with their formal education. The Yale Report of 1828 made a futile defense of the classical curriculum that emphasized mainly the "dead languages" as the best form of liberal learning for the college student with its focus only on Roman writers like Cicero, Tacitus, Livy, and others. But it was not until the antebellum college era, encompassing 1820 and 1860 that a more humanist curricular emphasis began to appear in college catalogs.

According to Caroline Winterer, the appeal in the United States for a more Greek or Hellenistic perspective in the college curriculum came from the German Romantic idealism of the early nineteenth century. Germany had found an affinity with Greek thought and literature, and this began to influence more Americans, especially those who had travelled to Germany for graduate level education. Thus, in the United States, "Professors who taught Demosthenes in their classroom after 1830 hoped that students would not just imitate his style but enter into his age . . . Ancient literature became incorporated into what George Marsden has called the 'liberal Protestantism' that would increasingly characterize the colleges after mid-century."[43] Eventually, the doors of the antebellum college classroom would open fully to more humanistic learning in poetry, drama, archeology, antiquities, biography, history, and modern literature. But it wasn't until President Charles Eliot enfranchised the elective course system at Harvard University that students there could choose the courses they, not the faculty, wanted to undertake.

As the modern era progressed, German research universities during the second half of the nineteenth century, under the

---

[43] Winterer, Caroline. The humanist revolution in America, 1820-1860: Classical antiquity in the colleges. *History of Higher Education Annual*, 18, 1998, p. 123.

educational philosophy of the freedom to teach and learn, expanded the potential and power for new thinking by demonstrating that existing knowledge should not only be preserved and disseminated but, through research and development new meaning and knowledge, can also be created and applied in the occupational setting. Johns Hopkins University would be established in 1876 as the first American institution dedicated only to graduate level education. The natural sciences, known in previous eras as natural philosophy, would emerge to initiate and inform what we currently call the applied sciences. The natural sciences would focus its scholarship and research efforts to discover the truths or laws of nature; however, empirically based results of many of these research efforts would continue to threaten, if not, discredit superstitious claims about why, for example, agriculture and weather patterns complemented each other during the different seasons of the year. The natural sciences include older subject matter such as astronomy, biology, and physics but would also later include earth sciences, oceanography, and, chemistry.

The most effective epistemological approach, commonly known as the scientific method, of this era would impact America's burgeoning research institutions, hasten the industrial revolution, and initiate the subsequent information technology age. As Western civilization advanced technologically and economically during the nineteenth century, the value of a liberal education came under increased criticism, and many deemed it anachronistic, if not irrelevant for modern society.

LIBERAL LEARNING QUESTIONED

Often, the case is made, however, that a humanities curricula does not speak to the needs of the "real world." This is not a recent argument as earlier concerns about what the purpose of a college education was supposed to be for society were posited by Latinist scholar F. W. Kelsey of the University of Michigan who argued in 1883 that society in his day "demands from our colleges something besides learning and culture. It calls for true men . . . who are earnest, and practical, who know something of the problems of real life."[44] Later in 1889, industrialists as famous as Andrew Carnegie stated, "While the college student has been learning . . . about a far distant past, or trying to master languages which are dead, such knowledge as seems adapted for life upon another planet . . . the future captain of industry is hotly engaged in the school of experience."[45]

Serving as economic and socio-cultural backdrop informing these comments during the late nineteenth century were a number of major civilizational dynamics in motion, including the advance of the Industrial Revolution in Britain and the United States but followed closely by Germany and Japan; the view among some elites that war could serve as a redemptive and invigorating experience for increasingly pampered men in American society, as exemplified by Theodore Roosevelt's explicit desire to fight in the Spanish-American War of 1898; the emergence of the United States as a credible world leader capable of projecting military power at will through a Mahanian naval power strategy designed to secure and maintain access to foreign markets; and a rising American middle-class more interested in "useful knowledge" than simply education in the philosophies, languages, and literature of the past.

In fact, it was earlier during the American Civil War, and in subsequent decades, that impetus for this type of thinking and expectation for useful knowledge was encouraged through the first (1862) and second (1890) Land Grant College Acts intended "to teach such branches of learning as are related to agriculture and the mechanic arts, in such manner as the legislatures of the States may respectively prescribe, in order to promote the liberal and practical education of the industrial classes in the several pursuits and professions in life."[46] The industrial classes wanted their desired

---

[44]   Kelsey, F. W. *The Study of Latin in Collegiate Education*. Education 3 (January 1883): p. 270.
[45]   Quoted in Allan Nevins. *The State of Universities and Democracy* (Urbana: University of Illinois Press. 1962), p. 35.
[46]   USC § 304. Investment of proceeds of sale of land or scrip.

form of college curricula to be viewed as valid but unique in the higher education sector as was the classical liberal arts curriculum; the latter set of curricula concentrated on the perennial ideas, history, and languages and the former on the emerging practical knowledge needs of the modern industrial world.

However, most traditionalists in the American academy during this period were not in favor of including what they perceived as only training for jobs and not true education for the work of life within traditional college offerings. In the end, it would also be the ancient traditional guardians of the queen of the sciences, the theological faculty, during the second half of the nineteenth century who would be largely abandoned by the natural philosophers (applied sciences), who instead wanted to search for agnostic truth using scientific methods and not continue to serve the interests of affirming man-made theological doctrines.

The American academy in the early twentieth century would become increasingly secular and pragmatic in the original sense but make attempts to rediscover, or give special attention to, the liberal arts and humanities as the General Honors curricula at Columbia University (1919), the Great Books program at the University of Chicago (1920s), or as outlined in the General Education in a Free Society Report released at Harvard University in 1945.

THE 1950S AND BEYOND

An interesting experiment occurred in 1952 at the Bell Telephone Company in Pennsylvania in relations to exposing sixteen promising executives possessing various formal education levels to a ten-month immersion program in the humanities through the University of Pennsylvania. After engaging various notable books, plays, works of art, and classical readings, there was *change* in the way many of these executives began to see their lives within the larger context of their communities. However, according to Davis,[47] "Bell gradually withdrew its support after yet another positive assessment found that while executives came out of the program more confident and more intellectually engaged, they were also less interested in putting the company's bottom line ahead of their commitments to their families and communities. By 1960, the Institute of Humanistic Studies for Executives was finished."

The decline in interest and perceived value of a liberal and humanities education would continue throughout the rest of the twentieth century as career-related curricula would ascend to new heights. The humanities would, nonetheless, experience a revival of sorts during and after the 1960s and 1970s social unrest periods; many ethnically underrepresented college students demanded and got increased diversity on the faculty and more courses in subject areas including women's studies, African-American studies, Jewish studies, Latino studies, Asian Studies, and others.

The Cold War would officially end in 1991, and as a consequence, many major institutions of higher learning would lose federal funding. What would replace federal dollars for many research universities would be new corporate-university joint research ventures; but the value of a liberal education would continue to be questioned and marginalized. The humanities, initiated during the Renaissance Period, still offers appeal to learners of all ages as it specifically concentrates on the arts and sciences of not the Creator but the creation; of utmost importance, the humanities promises to develop empathy for human and nonhuman creatures. This is important for both the bottom line at the largest multinational corporation and society as a whole.

---

[47]   Davis, Wes. "The 'Learning Knights' off Bell Telephone." *The New York Times*, Op-Ed Contributor, June 15, 2010.

CHAPTER 3

THE HUMANITIES: A WAY TO EMPATHY

*Anthropology is the most humanistic of the sciences
and the most scientific of the humanities.*

Alfred L. Kroeber (1876-1960)

🦉 🦉 🦉

Defining and differentiating what the humanities are from the natural, applied, and professional sciences has always been a challenge; the social sciences seem to be related to the humanities but are nonetheless a unique academic area. Most of what we would consider humanistic learning can be placed within the larger category of the "liberal arts." However, if humanities education is generally about the human condition on Earth, then it seems to me that those disciplinary areas that focus on hard scientific work and discoveries are not necessarily a part of humanistic learning disciplines.

Although increasingly, the emphasis in and outside of academe is on the need for more interdisciplinary collaboration between the arts and sciences, indeed, to understand more fully the human condition on Earth; thus, we can see a partnership between the Arts and Sciences (for example, art appreciation and biology) to create better understanding for an art therapist working in a psychiatric hospital ward. According to Stanford University's the Human Experience department, the humanities

> can be described as the study of the myriad ways in which people, from every period of history and from every corner of the globe, process and document the human experience. Since humans have been able, we have used philosophy, literature, religion, art, music, history and language to understand and record our world. These modes of expression have become some of the subjects that traditionally fall under the humanities umbrella. Knowledge of these records of human experience gives us the opportunity to feel a sense of connection to those who have come before us, as well as to our contemporaries.[48]

In the foregoing description of what can be considered the humanities, we can discern that it is through engagement in philosophy, literature, religion, art, music, history, and language that we connect with and experience the long human chain of being. In effect, learners are able to enter centuries-long dialogues and discussions with Plato, Hypatia, Descartes, Kant, Maya Angleou, Dostoyevsky, and others. The Humanities Education and Research Association (HERA) posits that the humanities covers a wider range of older and contemporary disciplines including:

- Ancient and modern languages and literatures, written or oral
- History
- Philosophy and religion
- The visual arts and architecture
- The performing arts, including theater, dance, and music

---

[48] "What are the humanities?" Stanford University the Human Experience. Web. 1 April 2014. (http://humanexperience.stanford.edu/what).

- Performing media, including film, television, and the Internet
- Related fields, such as archeology, anthropology, ethnic studies, women's studies, and history of science and engineering
- Those aspects of social sciences which have humanistic content and employ humanistic methods.

The HERA adds to the humanities list areas such as visual arts, architecture, theater, dance, music, film, the Internet, ethnic studies, gender studies, and even a hard science like engineering. It seems that human expression can be augmented by new forms of technology, such as television and the Internet. Indeed, the humanities have also expanded their focus to include historically marginalized classes of human experiences, like race, and gender, and sexual orientation.

As was highlighted in the previous chapter, during the early twentieth century, we saw the increased relevance and development of the humanities curricula, again, within the General Honors curricula at Columbia University (1919) and the Great Books program at the University of Chicago (1920s). One may speculate that perhaps these early programs were a response to an effort to prevent another "great war" between the super powers on earth, but this would not be so. The 1930s did provide, however, an opportunity for the emerging American civilization to deepen its exposer and commitment to the humanities. Many Americans would be exposed to what were considered "the humanities" through actual art, music, theater, and literature. The Great Depression of the 1930s would provide an opportunity for the nation to support the humanities in very interesting ways, in particular, through a variety of educational venues and programs. The federal government, through the Works Progress Administration, would take the lead but not without controversy.

THE HUMANITIES: FROM THE IVY
TOWER TO THE STREETS

The Great Depression of the 1930s was a time of economic, political, and cultural turmoil for the United States and much of the world. In the United States, the economic turmoil involved, among other things, an unemployment rate of roughly 25 percent during the worst stage of the 1930s; similar unemployment rates would also be reflected in other developed countries. Thus, many Americans during this era began to question the legitimacy of the free enterprise system and often flirted with the central planning model of the former Soviet Union which seemed to exemplify a type of economic stability. Politically, the United States remained true to its system of checks and balances, and this seemed to provide the nation with a kind of stability between the powers of the executive, judiciary, and the U.S. Congress. Within the cultural realm, the social contract between the American people and their government began to be rewritten.

The idea of the federal government using federal law or tax dollars to create and support programs, usually placed within the humanities or cultural categories, was new and controversial for many in and out of the U.S. government. But many in the Roosevelt administration (1933-1945) insisted that the government could affect positive economic, political, and cultural change in the nation during the Great Depression through specific and targeted government programs.

One such program was the Works Progress Administration's (WPA) Arts Program, known as Federal Program No. 1, enacted in 1935. One of the goals of this federal program was to employ artists, musicians, actors, and authors; the other major goal was to document the American experience, present and past, and ultimately enshrine the humanities' unique contribution to American history and cultural landscape. Thus, the goals of the WPA's Arts Program, that involved the Federal Arts Project, the Federal Music Program, the Federal Theater Project, and the

Federal Writer's Project, served to improve economic conditions for many in the country, and second, it supported the important goals of documenting American history as an important element of humanistic education.

FEDERAL ART PROJECT

The Federal Art Project was enacted in 1935 and terminated in 1939; the project's primary goal was to hire unemployed artists by leveraging a partnership involving the federal government and local municipalities to share the costs involved in paying artists' salaries and work supplies. Amy Trout writes that the various forms of art included murals, paintings, sculpture, educational materials, commemoratives, signs, ceramics, and stained glass. Other items include photographs documenting fine arts, art education, and the practical arts.

In an article titled *The Federal Art Project in New Haven: The Era, Art, & Legacy*, Trout explores one of the WPA's more successful art programs that involved a major educational institution, Yale University, and nearby municipalities, including New Haven, Hartford, and New London, Connecticut.[49] Apparently, the arts project leaders noticed that in Mexico during the 1920s a sense of national identity had been forged there as a result of key mural work completed in the public sphere by David Siquieros, Diego Rivera, and Jose Clemente Orozco.

In Connecticut, the WPA's art project leaders sought to depict and celebrate American history and key figures that represented colonial America. What is interesting to note is that of the forty-two U.S. artists, Theodore Sizer, PWAP administrator, records that he employed men where "22 were characterized as 'American,' 13 'Italian,' 3 'Polish,' 2 'German,' and 2 'Slavic.'" There were no African American or Native American artists employed, but a

---

[49] Trout, A. The Federal Art Project in New Haven: The Era, Art & Legacy. Hog River Journal, Vol. 5, No. 1, Winter 2006-2007.

few women, such as Lois North, Jeanette Brinsmade, Alexandra Darrows, and Lyndell Schwarz, would conduct much of their mural work within local high schools.

Be that as it may, some of the cultural themes celebrating American history included the *Daughters of the American Revolution* and colonial arts and architecture. The Federal Arts Program in Connecticut also celebrated local revolutionary war heroes, such as Roger Sherman, John Brockett, Nathan Hale, and others. Economic and industrial figures were also painted and displayed in public sector buildings. These included inventors such as Eli Whitney, Samuel Morse, and Thomas Sanford; hardware maker Joseph Sargent; clockmaker Chauncey Jerome; carriage maker James Brewster; and others. Thus, in Connecticut, the major themes emphasized and used to uplift their citizens' spirits during the Great Depression were murals reflecting historical revolutionary figures and themes, in addition to economic and industrial artifacts and luminaries. The historical and economic emphasis would be somewhat different in Cleveland, Ohio.

In a book entitled *The Federal Art Project in Cleveland* (1933-1943), Karal Marling (1974) celebrates the city's unique experience in leveraging its homegrown artistic talent, civic pride, and economic resources.[50] Marling provides an essay account of the unique mural projects accomplished through the WPA/FAP in Cleveland, Ohio. She also writes very cogently about the economic life of Cleveland during the worst part of the Great Depression. Indeed, she writes that the "rugged individualism" mindset of the time seemed to cause many Clevelanders to feel excessive shame for failing to meet their family and economic obligations.

The Cleveland Museum of Art's first director, William M. Milliken, who, after arriving from the U.S, Army in 1919, established the May Shows at the museum and made it clear that these shows and educational programs were to be accessible to all citizens and serve as sources of beauty, decoration, educational

---

[50]   Marling, K. A. FEDERAL ART IN CLEVELAND 1933-1943. The Board of Trustees, Cleveland Public Library, Cleveland: 1984.

value, and personal pleasure. While Marling's essay represents an authoritative and important personal account, there seems to be a lack of detachment to the topic that is often necessary for historical accounts to be considered objective and free of most personal bias.

Nonetheless, incredible art work and murals were completed in Cleveland reflecting contrasting themes such as William Summer's *Farms,* Clarence Carter's *Bridges,* and John Csosz's *Early and Modern Scenes from Ohio History* reflecting some of Ohio's economic resources; the former seems to celebrate Ohio's rural farming heritage and the two latter themes the industrial and scientific accomplishments achieved through bridge structures and the aviation industry. One particular mural painted by Russell Limbach, titled *Laying the Cornice stone of the Cleveland Post Office,* depicts three common working men, not wearing any salient status symbols, placing the post office's cornerstone in place; this mural would seem to advance masonic allegories about the brotherhood of men meeting *on the level* to accomplish great things.

And yet other watercolor sketches would be placed in public schools such as Gladys Carambella's *Thumbellina #3* or William Krusoe's *The Spirit of Education* mural that was painted at Lincoln Junior High School. At the end of this federal project, the federal government directed the states that the various art forms produced through the WPA/FAP be allocated to tax-supported public institutions. In addition to art projects, the WPA also supported music programs across the nation.

FEDERAL MUSIC PROJECT

In a brief article titled *Federal Music Project,* Craig H. Roell (2013) reveals that during the Great Depression years, roughly 60 percent of formerly employed musicians were unemployed by 1934 as compared to 25 percent of the U.S. population at large.[51] Nikolai Sokoloff became the national director for the Federal Music Project (FMP). Reoll's article focuses on the State of Texas but points out that it was a part of the FMP's Region 8, which, for program funding purposes, also included states like Oklahoma, Arkansas, and Louisiana.

While Sokoloff served as national director of the FMP, coordination and funding control was accomplished locally through city councils, school boards, chambers of commerce, universities, musician's unions, and the Texas Federation of Music Clubs. Cities including San Antonio, Dallas, Fort Worth, and El Paso received funding for copying and transcribing of Spanish, Mexican, and unique Cuban folk music indigenous to the State of Texas. Much credit has been given to local Texas FMP leaders like Ms. Lucil Lyons of Fort Worth for funding culturally diverse musical genres at a time in Texas where centuries-long Latino residents were being told to "go back to Mexico."

Walker Moore also would direct operas and choral performances in Fort Worth involving music that was common to the national American character. Ultimately, Roell asserts that the FMP trained thousands of musicians throughout Texas, which included children and rural residents. In fact, one of the key consequences of the FMP was its ability to uplift the morale of countless Americans across many cities throughout Texas and Region 8. This included African Americans in Texas but mostly in the American South and Northeast.

In a book entitled *More Than Dancing, Essays on Afro-American Music and Musicians,* various essays are published which highlight the various humanities programs ascribed to African American

---

[51] Roell, C. H. (2013). FEDERAL MUSIC PROJECT. Handbook of Texas Online. Web. 1 Nov 2013. (http://www.tshaonline.org/handbook/online/articles/xmf01).

culture.[52] For instance, in her chapter essay titled *The Music Program of the Works Progress Administration: A Documentation and Description of Its Activities with Special Reference to Afro-Americans,* Lorraine M. Faxio (1985) writes about how "Afro Americans" specifically benefited from the WPA's Federal Music Program across many U.S. cities during the Great Depression. In fact, African Americans found new opportunities to appear in operas such as Verdi's *Trovatore* in New York and *Fra Diavole* in Los Angeles. Moreover, "In North Carolina, music productions successfully joined Black and White musicians" (Faxio, p. 245). In fact, Nell Hunter, a black teacher and choral director, stated, "All seem to catch the spirit of harmony that, to my mind, is the primary mission of music." (Faxio, p. 245); Plato would say as much in his *Republic.*

Faxio's work would also address the shift in priorities that occurred once Sokoloff was replaced by Earl Moore as national director of the FMP in 1939. Basically, Sokoloff's emphasis on performance and symphonies was replaced by a new commitment to music education and community service; thus, teaching about music and offering band clinics became a priority in many communities such as Atlanta, Washington DC, New York, and others. The WPA's national administrators also found it important to fund programs in theater across the country.

FEDERAL THEATER PROJECT

In a book entitled *FURIOUS IMPROVISATION: How the WPA and a Cast of Thousands Made High Art out of Depression Times,* Susan Quinn (2008) provides a vivid account in what is considered the most recent book on the Federal Theater Project

---

[52] Faxio, L. M. The Music Program of the Works Progress Administration: A Documentation and Description of Its Activities with Special Reference to Afro-Americans. In Ed. I. V. Jackson, *More Than Dancing: Essays on Afro-American Music and Musicians.* Westport: Greenwood Press, 1985, pp. 239-269.

(FTP).[53] Many of the theater productions funded by the WPA's theater project addressed controversial issues. Quinn highlights some the major figures involved in some of these theatrical productions, including Orson Welles, Sinclair Lewis, and John Houseman.

In particular, it was important to highlight the NTP's national director's, Hallie Flanagan, commitment to social and racial justice in one of the book's chapters; in this account, a freshman student committee of Grinnell College is having trouble inviting a matriculated black student to the freshmen party. Flanagan, appalled by the apparent comfort with the intended discrimination, decides to "go to the party with him" in spite of one of the male committee member's comments that he wouldn't go out with a girl who had dated a black male. Flanagan would have many enemies throughout her life according to Quinn, but belonging to an often discriminated group herself, an Irish American, it is safe to assume that Flanagan was able to empathize with African Americans at some credible level. Her commitment to racial justice would be manifested in the FTP's support of African American theater in the State of Washington.

In an article titled *The Federal Theater Project in Washington State,* Sara Guthu (2009) writes about the participation of African Americans in theater productions through the Seattle Negro Repertory Company; these productions were enthusiastically supported by the FTP national director Hallie Flanagan. In particular, the article points out that the various theatrical productions offered through the FTP in Washington State provided an opportunity for actors to perform their talents while also addressing controversial social and racial issues. Theatrical productions were not only offered within metropolitan areas like Seattle. Due to the Civilian Conservation Corp's (CCC) rural work

---

[53] Quinn, S. *FURIOUS IMPROVISATION: How the WPA and a Cast of Thousands Made High Art Out of Depression Times.* New York: Walker & Company, 2008. Print.

locations, administrators believed it was important for FTP-funded theatrical productions be offered to CCC workers.

According to Guthu, FTP administrators also were strongly interested in creating a new generation of theater goers; perhaps FTP leaders believed that exposing a new generation of theater goers to quality plays would make this art form sustainable, economically and culturally, once the Great Depression was over. Ultimately, Flannigan would create a new scriptwriters competition for playwrights who had never launched a play on Broadway in New York; the winner would receive $250 and a two-week run on Broadway. The WPA also would launch the Federal Writers Project in an effort to document American history and experience during the Great Depression.

FEDERAL WRITERS PROJECT

The WPA/FWP would support unique and crucial writing efforts designed to document and archive important American history by hiring thousands of unemployed writers and librarians. The slave narratives would relate to southern living and history, in particular, the relationship between black slaves and white plantation owners. In an online anthology, history professor Bruce Fort (1996) of the University of Virginia archived firsthand accounts of slave life from the former slave themselves.[54] In general, the slave narratives address compelling themes, including labor, resistance and flight, relations with plantation owners, family life, and religious and spiritual beliefs.

By clicking at the "annotated index of narrative" link, the reader is ushered into a page of other hyperlinks containing the particular slave narratives. Some of them reflect the violent experiences of the black slave. For instance, Charity Anderson from

---

[54] Bruce, F. American Slave Narratives: An Online Anthology, Summer 1996. Web. 1 Nov 2013. (http://xroads.virginia.edu/~hyper/wpa/index. html).

Alabama spoke about watching some slaves being torn up by dogs or whipped unmercifully; Emma Crockett sang her favorite hymn in spite of her headache during her interview; Lucinda Davis, a product of a Creek Indian father and white mother, recalled Creek funerals, dances, and food recipes. As far as men were concerned, the narratives include stories from Walter Calloway from Virginia. Walter recalled witnessing a girl being whipped close to death and federal troops ransacking the plantation he worked in after the Civil War ended.

Fort includes Richard Toker's account as well; Richard was a slave in Virginia and tended to cows, learned blacksmithing, and became an accomplished musician by the end of his life. One narrative involved the life and marriage of Mrs. Tempe H. Durham. She describes the stoop labor experienced by many slaves required to plant and harvest corn, wheat, cotton, and tobacco. Mrs. Durham also describes her wedding day to Mr. Exter Durham "on the front porch of the master's home." She and her husband would save enough money to buy their own home once they retired, thus achieving a form of freedom most slaves could only dream of during this time. Oftentimes, the writer's project would be accused of being a haven for those with communist sympathies.

In an article titled *Unmasking Writers of the W.P.A.,* David Brinkley (August 2, 2003)[55] writes about noted luminaries like John Cheevers and Ralph Ellison, the latter the author of the *Invisible Man.* Indeed, he writes that the WPA writer's project was where social and economic history served to prick individuals' imagination with important and controversial literature; this literature addressed issues of class, race, gender, economics, culture, and even the KKK in Florida. Brinkley quotes American filmmaker Andrea Kalin: "The W.P.A. is much more than guidebooks and oral histories, . . . It was where social and economic history met the individual imagination in literature" (p. A15). As some of these writer's works would highlight the many contradictions

---

[55]   Brinkley, D. *Unmasking Writers of the W.P.A.* The New York Times, August 02, 2003, A15.

encountered in American life about social and economic injustice, many politicians would accuse the FWP's administrators of being in sympathy with socialist or communist goals. He mentions specifically a Democratic politician from Texas who accuses the WPA of being an actual communist plot designed to undermine the American way of life.

Within the WPA's Federal Writing Project, administrators also intended to initiate or encourage literacy, especially in rural communities where libraries and basic literacy were many times lacking. One such effort was the WPA's Rural Libraries Program.

In an article titled *WPA and Rural Libraries,* Edward Chapman (October 1, 1938) writes about particular statewide rural library services, headed by Ellen S. Woodward, that would focus on three states, namely South Carolina, Ohio, and Kentucky. For instance, in Ohio, Chapman describes the statewide program where specific counties would be combined and supported through regional and statewide library associations. Of critical importance in Ohio was the continued funds support from the state legislature. In Kentucky, the workers would find themselves having to penetrate very rural regions and experiencing suspicion by some of the residents. Indeed, a general mistrust on the part of rural Kentucky residents of outside help had to be overcome in order to make marginal progress. Due to the lack of sufficient transportation infrastructure, the "Pack-horse library service" was only offered within the southeastern part of the state.

Chapman writes that in places like South Carolina and others, churches and clubs seemed to be the only repositories of books, most of which were donations. Magazines like *Popular Mechanics* and nonfiction titles seemed to be more popular. However, by far, the most popular reading materials were children's books, and these were demanded by children and adults alike.

The proceeding accounts outline how the Works Progress Administration contributed to the well-being of many communities in the country; this was accomplished by initiating, sustaining, or expanding the humanities educational value in American life during the Great Depression of the 1930s. Indeed, the WPA

Arts Program served to improve economic conditions for many, including artists, musicians, writers, sculptors, and others; many of these programs, designed to employ artists and writers, would also indirectly benefit, economically and morale-wise, the very communities in which the work was being accomplished.

Moreover, many of the themes and subject matter depicted in murals, in music, or in written narratives documented and archived important American history like the slave narratives. And yet other books such as the *Grapes of Wrath, Of Mice and Men*, and literature appropriate to children enhanced literacy, sensitized more Americans about social justice, refuted fascist ideologies, and enhanced the importance of literacy in the nation; essentially, the history and literature that was being documented and disseminated served a crucial educational mission for the times. While the WPA would be dissolved in June of 1943, its legacy would eventually be replaced in 1965 by the National Endowment for the Arts. Its mission statement says: "The NEA is dedicated to supporting excellence in the arts, both new and established; bringing the arts to all Americans; and providing leadership in arts education." Many forms of literature have informed, inspired, and educated the individual about the natural world and different people alike. However, its deeper purpose in the free society is the intentional development of empathy for human and nonhuman creations.

LITERACY, LITERATURE, AND EMPATHY

In a play titled *The Mourning Bride* (1697), Almeria in Act I, Scene 1 succinctly states that "music has charms to soothe the savage breast, to soften rocks, or bend a knotted oak"; basically, music can have the power to calm some of the fear-based primal impulses that many humans tend to be born with or cultivate in life. Literacy, simply understood to be the ability to read and write, can also contribute to a deeper level of soothing, softening, and bending of our souls to better understand and empathize with the people and world around us.

Works of literature, especially those considered lasting and influential, take the young reader in school or college into the lives and human journeys they may relate to or never get to experience themselves; and we hope that they not only acquire understanding about *others* but also develop a level of empathy for others' trials, tribulations, and triumphs. Thus, being literate and engaging at deeper levels of understanding of good literature contributes to what it generally means to be a literate citizen in our world. Journal articles and books have been written about the connection between literacy, great literature, and the development of humanistic or empathetic, engagement in society among young students. Therefore, strong literary reading habits can contribute to the development of the individual's, adolescent or older, positive character traits, confidence in expressing emotional responses to an author's ideas, genuine empathy about others' experiences and ideas, and a commitment to active citizenship engagement with her or his community at wider scales.

According to Merriam-Webster (2013),[56] *literature* can be defined as "writings in prose or verse; *especially*: writings having excellence of form or expression and expressing ideas of permanent or universal interest." So, defined as such, literature, in forms of textbooks, novels, short stories, essays, poetry, or plays, carries perennial ideas and philosophies that have a personal, and sometimes professional, appeal to the human spirit or mind.

Intentional and purposeful engagement with many forms of literature can develop a student's level of empathy about his or her social context. In an article titled *Implications of Civility for Children and Adolescents: A Literature Review*, Wilkins, Caldarella, Crook-Lyon, and Young (2012) write about the early efforts in American schools to develop in adolescents certain character traits conducive to empathetic action, civil behavior toward others, and citizenship activities in the community.[57]

---

[56] "Literature." Merriam-Webster Dictionary. Web. 1 Nov 2013.

[57] Wilkins, K., Caldarella, P., Crook-Lyon, R., Young, K. Implications of Civility for Children and Adolescents: A Review of the Literature. *Issues in Religion and Psychotherapy*, North America, 33, Jan. 2011.

Wilkins et al. state that starting in the 1830s, the McGuffey Readers essentially served to help adolescents learn how to read while using idioms or sayings relating to civility. These readers emphasized moral integrity, character, ethical conduct, individual responsibility, and acceptable social demeanor; additional topics discussed by teachers and students included diligence, politeness, negotiation, respect for others, and other personal traits. While Wilkins et al. outline how effective the McGuffey Readers were in acculturating certain moral traits, the article does not address how church Sunday school programs or other secular private school curricula educated for similar human traits conducive to the development of empathy. At this stage of literacy development, students tend to experience literature largely as a passive recipient of others' ideas. Others, including Eileen M. Burke, have written about the literary needs of adolescents, especially as it relates to achieving the necessary response to literature.

In her book entitled *Literature for the Young*, Burke (1990) writes that literature belongs in the lives of children as it enables them to access a wide range of knowledge about the world to experience a diversity of emotions, in addition to stimulating further curiosity and reflective thinking.[58] In this book, Burke segments some of the experiential dimensions of literature in an adolescent's education, including the use of story sharing as a link to literacy; discussing the feel of literature and the sound of literature, such as poetry, song, and laughter; or exploring what the sight of literature can be, literature about the past and present, and the facts of informational literature are crucial dimensions to explore.

Burke asserts further that teachers must recognize the point at which children engage the story within literature. For instance, stories which appeal to adolescent's emotions tend to achieve better response and connection over the long run. In Chapter 11 of the book, Burke writes that there are several examples of literature

---

[58] Burke, Eileen M. *Literature For The Young* (2nd Ed.). Boston: Allyn and Bacon, 1990.

that can achieve rich responses by adolescents. For example, classroom activities involving Forrest Wilson's *How Does It Feel to Be a Building* can help with dramas, or Arthur Yorinks's *Hey, Al!* can supplement sculpting art activities; using Russell Hoban's *France's* to produce new music or discussing what Carlo Collodi's *Pinocchio's* means when it comes to telling lies or the truth to others can produce better response and deeper involvement in literary experiences. While Burke argues effectively for appealing to adolescents' emotions, she does not seem to address the issue of levels of emotional maturity and the types of reading materials that may be off limits to adolescents. Others like Louis M. Rosenblatt believed that at some point in intellectual development, a reader's emotional responses to the text should also be taken into consideration by teachers.

In her seminal work *Literature as Exploration,* Rosenblatt (1995) establishes what we now know as the reader-response theory.[59] Through this theory, Rosenblatt argues that teachers should be aware of the relationship occurring between a student's emotions and the text he or she is engaging with. She asserts that a *transactional* relationship, that is, a two-way reciprocal hermeneutical dynamic involving a student and a piece of literature, can develop, and as such, a reader's emotional engagement should be read as carefully as the book itself by teachers during literary discussions.

Rosenblatt further writes that the literature teacher not only should disseminate science-based information but also engender the habits of thinking that are helpful toward deeper social understanding in the world. Rosenblatt argues that an English teacher has the opportunity to play a crucial role in a student's positive social adjustment and this at a deeper level through the transactional engagement with literature. For instance, in the chapter addressing the issue of personality, Rosenblatt argues that literature can serve as a role model in the process of assimilating

---

[59]   Rosenblatt, Louise M. *Literature as exploration.* New York: Modern Language Association of America, 1995.

some of the character traits of the various lives encountered in a novel, a biography, or a drama. Rosenblatt cites works like *War and Peace* or *Human Comedy* as examples of panoramic sociological narratives about human relationships.

Or as it relates to the life experience of a young man or racial injustice, works like *A Portrait of the Artist as a Young Man* and *Invisible Man* can produce sensitivity about the fleeting nature of life or the need to positively affirm all of humanity around us. Ultimately, she writes that as the proliferation of literacy and books continues, there is the potential for literature to play an increasingly crucial role in the further assimilation of super-arching attitudes that are more so based on basic human tendencies or impulses common to all. Others like psychologist and professor Steven Pinker at Harvard University would agree with Rosenblatt.

In a book entitled *The Better Angels of Our Nature: Why violence has declined,* Steven Pinker (2011), a leading authority on language and the mind, conducted a longitudinal study encompassing fifty centuries of global human history; his study focused particularly on the patterns of human violence during this time-frame.[60] Contrary to popular accounts in the media and elsewhere, Pinker's empirical findings actually point to the fact that we live in a more peaceful world due, in part, to the improvement in the legal system and in the wider spread of literacy.

Indeed, Pinker argues that the greater the understanding of others through literature, the less violence there tends to be in society; in fact, it was through the increased ability to read and write that political authorities were able to make and spread a common law system that tended to reduce, if not, prevent, for instance, domestic violence. Pinker points to the power of poetry and the novel as key literary forms which tend to contribute to the reduction of harmful actions and social injustice; particular novels such as Rousseau's *Julia* and Richard's *Pamela* gave insights into the lives and encouraged compassion for those without power, including servants, children, and women.

---

[60]   Pinker, Steven. *The Better Angels of our Nature.* New York: Viking, 2011.

Pinker argues effectively about the role of literacy and education in reducing the level of violence in Western society, but what he does not seem to credit are the influences of the increase in interracial marriage patterns where at least two cultures often meet to understand more about each other. Moreover, the improvement in cross-border trade and commerce has also had a positive effect on the reduction of violence between democratic societies. Elaine Scarry argues that thinking of empathy in more than one way is important to the spread of normative ethics and social justice.

In a journal article titled *The Literacy Revolution: Poetry, Injury, and the Ethics of Reading,* Scarry begins her analysis by asking the question: *what is the ethical power of literature?*[61] Scarry credits the greater emphasis in human empathy on the development of the Humanitarian Revolution of the modern era. She agrees with Pinker that literature does develop empathy but not the kind we expect when we read about a character's plight in a novel. Instead, she describes a different kind of empathy that literature can engender, specifically, as the capacity to recognize that there are other points of view in the world that must be factored into our habits of thinking; thus, the idea is that not only is it important to develop and exercise affective empathy but also intellectual empathy about what others think. And yet other reports have investigated literary reading's impact not only on the personal and intermediate levels but also within wider social contexts.

In a report titled *Reading at Risk: A Survey of Literary Reading in America* (2004), the National Endowment for the Arts (NEA) sounded the alarm about the dramatic decline in readership among all demographic groups in American society during the last quarter of the twentieth century. In particular, however, the NEA report outlined the wider social involvement habits of literary readers in other leisure and cultural events in their communities. According to this report, readers are highly social individuals who frequent sporting events, art exhibits, volunteer more and participate in

---

[61]   Scarry, Elaine. *The Literacy Revolution.* Boston Review, Jul/Aug 2012, Vol. 37 Issue 4, pp. 66-70, 5p.

community events at higher rates than nonreaders; thus, literary readers tend to exhibit higher levels of diverse social engagement in their communities and often abroad.

For instance, literary readers are three times as likely to attend performing arts events, nearly four times as likely to attend museums displaying art exhibits, over one-and-a-half times more likely to attend and/or participate in sporting events, and over two-and-a-half times as likely to accomplish volunteer or charity work compared to nonliterary readers.

Additionally, the report indicated that during the twelve-month period ending in August 2012, 49 percent of literary readers attended a performing arts event as compared to only 17 percent of nonreaders. Moreover, only 12 percent of nonreaders were likely to attend an art museum as compared to literary readers (44 percent). With respect to citizenship, the report also outlined that, during 2002, those who did not read literature were less involved in volunteering and charity work (17 percent) as compared to literary readers (43 percent). Others argue for the idea that reading can accomplish more than simply the acquisition of facts; reading can engender a social compact between the literary reader and his or her community, often leading to much needed humanitarian citizenship for the benefit of others.

In his book entitled *Readicide, How Our Schools Are Killing Reading and What You Can Do About It,* Gallagher (2009) supports the idea of what one of his colleagues, Robert J. Sternberg, calls "expert citizens."[62] Gallagher and Sternberg support the idea that literacy should focus not only on the acquisition of facts but most especially on expert citizen traits as well, such as common sense, wisdom, creativity, ethics, honesty, teamwork, hard work, knowing how to win and lose, and a sense of fair play. Gallagher writes that expert citizens can also be characterized as engaged, creatively flexible, and able to think critically about the information provided to them by various influential sources in society.

---

[62] Gallagher, Kelley. *Readicide: How schools are killing reading and what you can do about it.* Portland: Stenhouse Publishers, 2009.

Students can also develop empathy for the oppressed and marginalized in society according to Gallagher. For instance, Gallagher writes that novels, such as Harper Lee's *To Kill a Mockingbird*, can be used to examine racism in the world; or perhaps the book entitled *Of Mice and Men* can sensitize many about the challenges faced by itinerant migrant workers and those with mental and emotional disabilities who are often marginalized by society or considered the outcast in the world. The use by teachers and students in the learning environment of key works of literature, therefore, can help in the development of the aforementioned humanistic traits.

However, what Gallagher and others in the teaching profession disagree with immensely are the overbearing state-mandated teaching standards that tend to interfere with the goals of literacy and the potential for the subsequent appreciation of great literature in the classroom. According to Gallagher, the too-numerous teaching standards imposed upon teachers in the classroom, in effect, eliminate much of the required time it takes for students and teachers to more deeply analyze important texts, many of which that inform better citizenship traits in students and later in life; thus, there is less time to experience what Rosenblatt called "reader-response" in the classroom.

In a subsequent report titled *To Read or Not To Read A Question of National Consequence* (2007), the National Endowment for the Arts (NEA) also analyzed the connection between good readers and citizenship. Within the section of "Readers serve the Communities," this NEA report's findings indicate that volunteering was the civic activity most tracked by the Endowment's survey. For example, the report indicates that 43 percent of literary readers volunteered or accomplished acts of charity as compared to 16 percent of nonreaders; indeed, it was generally the case across all demographic groups that literary readers volunteered at markedly higher rates than nonreaders. As it relates to literary readers, interest levels in voting, current events, public affairs, and the government, the report makes explicit certain associations. For instance, voting activity is higher

(84 percent) among those who have higher reading skill levels as compared to those (53 percent) with lower reading skill levels.

Under the section titled "Reading as an Act of Empathy," this NEA report briefly explores the question of what may account for the differences between individuals with high/low reading ability and their general patterns of civic engagement. The report speculates that lower reading individuals, who are also of lower income generally have a lack of time, often live in bad neighborhoods or suffer from bad health; and thus, these factors may be preventing them from experiencing citizenship in more enriching ways, especially by engaging in volunteering or other acts of empathy in their community.

This section of the report also quotes the famous novelist and theologian C.S. Lewis to make the case for the positive association between readers and their fellow human beings. Lewis writes:

> Literary experience heals the wound, without undermining the privilege, of individuality. There are mass emotions which heal the wound; but they destroy the privilege . . . . But in reading great literature I become a thousand men and yet remain myself . . . . Here, as in worship, in love, in moral action, and in knowing, I transcend myself; and am never more myself than when I do.

In this quote, Lewis emphasizes that through great literature we can experience many more lives than we could ever live without *losing* our own identity. Indeed, this NEA report asserts that, while good readers are better able to appreciate the outlook of the *other,* all the while the individual reader is also *enlarging* their own identity in the educational process. What the report fails to address, however, is that there still remains disproportionate access by various cultural and socio-economically disadvantaged communities in the nation; therefore, low income communities with lower tax bases have access to, at best, outdated information technology tools for Internet access or outdated library facilities.

As such, there is very little social capital acquired or developed in families across many communities.

SUMMARY

Several writers have argued and demonstrated that literacy competency and its application to socially important examples of literature are important to the intellectual and ethical development of adolescents and older students. Again, children can respond and achieve better connections to literature when their emotions also are appealed to by various storyline and visual accounts; an adolescent's ability to "feel for" another often begins when teachers consider how a book can relate to children's affective dimension so as to achieve, at least sympathy, with story characters. However, as adolescents grow in age, it is also important to recognize their emotional responses to literature; thus, the emotional response of the reader must also be "read" by teachers when discussing important literature in the learning environment.

Longitudinal studies conducted by academics like Steven Pinker at Harvard University have affirmed the notion that improved literacy and wider access to education involving important literature and informational texts has contributed to better laws that tend to prevent violence, such as domestic and street-level violence; moreover, due to increased understanding and empathy of the "other," often achieved through interactional literary reading experiences, cross-cultural *faux pas*, economic tension, and war between nations have lessened. Others like Scarry have also affirmed literacy's power to not only develop emotional empathy for others but also intellectual empathy for others' ideas, and thus, their perspectives are recognized as important to consider; this presumably has the potential for decreasing what is known as egocentricity in persons who naturally want to get their own way or be right always.

Thus, effective literacy and the influencing power of important literature can produce a type of citizen, what Gallagher calls an *expert citizen*, who can empathize with others and engage critically and creatively in the wider social and cultural life of their communities. His ideas were affirmed by the National Endowment for the Art's (NEA) report about *To Read Or Not To Read*.

In this NEA report, researchers were keen on conveying the strong connections between high literary readers and their social commitment to the wellbeing of their communities. The subsequent NEA report titled *Reading on the Rise* does report more positive news about new trends in the appreciation for better reading habits in the country.[63] The hope is that with this renewed effort on reading, an emphasis on reading for empathy development among males in particular is also made. While reading habits in longer narratives, such as novels or biographies, have always been strong for young women, young men have tended to prefer shorter informational texts like magazines, manuals, comic books, and others; this has tended to prevent the development of social and interpersonal empathy among many young men. However, Charles Darwin's reading of Alexander von Humboldt's long *Personal Narrative* about the latter's travels and research in the Western Hemisphere is one example of how literature can change the course of one person's life and the world for men and women alike.

We can also take competency in literary understanding to different levels. Some of the most influential writing was accomplished by the likes of Alexander von Humboldt and his quasi-protégé Charles Darwin during the early nineteenth century. By comparing what each writer stated about similar phenomena, we can begin to discern the interesting way that scientists' narratives actually inform new research foci or to confirm or deny the validity of initial narrative accounts.

Comparing the writing styles of Alexander von Humboldt and Charles Darwin can be an interesting challenge, but it also can offer insights into how two natural scientists experienced voyages

---

[63] National Endowment for the Arts. *Reading on the rise: A new chapter in American Literacy.* Washington: National Endowment for the Arts, 2009. Web. 1 Aug 2013 (http://www.nea.gov/pub/pubLit.php.).

involving similar ecological and cultural locales; indeed, they both blend accounts of humanistic and natural sciences interest. Of course, Humboldt would precede Darwin, but both would encounter and write about similar ecological and climate conditions in South America. What follows is an exploration of the similar and dissimilar writing styles of both Humboldt and Darwin as they both write about earthquakes and the general atmospheric conditions of the tropical regions of South America.

EARTHQUAKES AND RAIN

Humboldt's book entitled *Personal Narrative of a Journey to the Equinoctial Regions of the New Continent* (1837) would provide many in the Old World with exciting but important scientific insights about many of the ecological and cultural environments he encountered in the Western Hemisphere; the years encompassed within this narrative include 1799-1804. One of the figures who would read *The Narrative* was Charles Darwin, author of the *The Voyage of the Beagle* that was published in 1839. There were two particular topics, among many, wherein both Humboldt and Darwin commented on in their writings, the latter referencing the former in one case; these two topics include earthquakes and tropical climates. With regards to earthquakes, Humboldt writes:

> In Caracas, and for 90 leagues around, not one drop of rain had fallen for five months up to the destruction of the capitol. The 26th of March was a very hot day: there was no wind and no cloud. It was Ascension Day and most people had congregated in the churches. Nothing suggested the horrors to come. At seven minutes past four the first shock was felt . . . . 'The shocks coming from these contrary movements tore the city apart.

Thousands of people were trapped in the churches and homes."[64]

In the foregoing account, Humboldt's writing style reflects two approaches. He uses very precise descriptions to weave his narrative including statements like "90 leagues around," "not one drop of rain," "a very hot day," and "seven minutes past four." Humboldt also uses a quotation derived from a manuscript written by DelPeche to fill out this account.

As it relates to content, he follows the example of M. de la Condamine, who wrote about the tremors and eruptions of Cotopaxi long after his departure from South America. However, Humboldt makes no association between a rainy season and earthquake events in Caracas; Darwin broaches this same topic in his own book *The Voyage of the Beagle* but documents this phenomenon in a different way. Darwin writes:

> The connexion between earthquakes and the weather has been often disputed; . . . Humboldt has remarked in one part of the Personal Narrative (Vol. iv. p. 11 and vol. ii p. 217), that it would be difficult for any person who had long resided in New Andalusia, or in Lower Peru, to deny that there exists some connexion between these phenomena; in another part, however, he seems to think the connexion fanciful. At Guayaquil, it is said that a heavy shower in the dry season is invariably followed by an earthquake . . . . I was much struck by this, when mentioning to some people at Copiapo that there had been a sharp shock at Coquimbo: they immediately cried out, 'How fortunate! There will be plenty of pasture there this year.'"[65]

---

[64] Von Humboldt, Alexander. *Personal Narrative of a Journey to the Equinoctial Regions of the New Continent.* London, England: Penguin Books, 1995, p. 141. Print.

[65] Darwin, Charles. *The Voyage of the Beagle.* New York: Everyman's Library, 2003, p. 363. Print.

A part of Darwin's writing style is to ground his topical focus on what Humboldt said about earthquakes. Darwin states that many believe heavy showers during the dry season are usually followed by an earthquake. Indeed, instead of quoting DelPeche's written manuscript as Humboldt has, Darwin quotes the words of some of the actual residents of Copiapo; according to Darwin, "To their minds an earthquake foretold rain, as surely as rain foretold abundant pasture" (363). Darwin seems hesitant to posit any of his own thoughts about a very dubious relationship between rain and earthquakes.

The other ecological topic addressed by both Humboldt and Darwin was about tropical climates. Darwin writes:

> It may be observed that the houses within the tropics are surrounded by the most beautiful forms of vegetation . . . During this day I was particularly struck with a remark of Humboldt's, who often alludes to 'the thin vapour which, without changing the transparency of the air, renders its tints more harmonious, and softens its effects.' This is an appearance I have never observed in the temperate zones."[66]

In the foregoing account, Darwin refuses to affirm Humboldt's account regarding the supposed vapor conditions within this tropical zone. Thus, he uses Humboldt's own words to contrast his own experience within this region; in effect, Darwin's writing style adds more detail about the ecological context, stating instead that "the atmosphere . . . was perfectly lucid, but at a greater distance all colours were blended into a most beautiful haze . . ." (46). Perhaps both descriptions are fine and not necessarily in stark disagreement, but they offer different perspectives of the same thing and this is in accord with the preferences of the Age of Romanticism where it was no longer just one authority defining the actual experience. Humboldt suggests as much when he writes:

---

[66] Ibid. p. 46. Print.

When a traveller recently arrived from Europe steps
into South American jungle for the first time he sees
nature in a completely *unexpected* guise . . . . If he is
able to *feel* the beauty of landscape, he will find it hard
to *analyse* his many impressions." (italics mine). [67]

In the foregoing quote, Humboldt not only suggests that a
traveler to South America will have diverse impressions about the
jungle there; this will apply to the impressions others will have
of the same places. Moreover, he suggests that the affective (feel)
dimension may interfere with the cognitive (analyze) dimension as
he or she attempts to produce a sound impression of the ecological
environment. Humboldt's writing style above contrasts both the
dimensions of heart and mind, in addition to European civilization
and South American jungles.

FINDINGS

Humboldt and Darwin's writing styles are similar in that they
both use very precise terms and language about the environments
they interacted with; with the exception of temperature ranges,
there seems to be very little evidence of other technical or scientific
terms and data used in both narratives. This seeming similarity, I
believe, is one way that Humboldt influenced Darwin's thinking
and writing in *The Voyage of the Beagle*. Darwin also employs
quotations but does so by using others' actual words in contrast
to Humboldt, who used direct quotes from actual written sources.

Darwin used Humboldt's own words to, in fact, disagree with
him about the ecological character of tropical lands. Thus, it is
evident to me that, at least within these two written excerpts, that
these two contemporaries knew of each other's work; but Darwin
used Humboldt's narrative accounts to gain initial inspiration and
insights about South America, its cultures, ecology, and social

---

[67] Ibid. p. 83.

institutions to engage in better research of his own leading to the theory of evolution.

Another literary development approach requires creativity rooted in actual nonfictional accounts. Roger McDonald would use Charles Darwin's writings not to inform his own voyage originally chartered by the former but to create a new story surrounding actual characters involved in Darwin's voyage on the H.M.S. *Beagle*; the new fiction book would focus not on Darwin but on Syms Covington, his humble assistant.

A MODERN CREATION

Writing a fictional account from nonfictional sources seems to require closer dependence and support from the actual events and people originally involved; not closely aligning to the original true story would perhaps render any new account as simply a new fiction book. Thus, it seems that when writing *Mr. Darwin's Shooter,* Roger McDonald was much indebted to original primary and secondary sources as root sources that informed much of his conceptual approach to the novel. This section will argue that McDonald used primary and secondary sources, imagination, fictional techniques, formative imagination, personal interpretation, and his own feelings to convert factual records into the fiction book entitled *Mr. Darwin's Shooter.*

FORMAL SOURCES

So what were some of the sources used by McDonald to write *Mr. Darwin's Shooter?*[68] McDonald (1998) begins disclosing his primary and secondary sources at the end of this book within the "author's note" section beginning on page 363. He writes, "For Covington I used all of the above except the first," meaning that

---

[68] McDonald, Roger. *Mr Darwin's shooter.* London: Anchor, 1998.

his literary sources included *The Red Notebook of Charles Darwin* (1980), *The Correspondence of Charles Darwin, Volume I, 1821-1836 and Volume II*, and, finally, *Charles Darwin's Beagle Diary* (1988) but not the *Origin of Species*. McDonald also used an unpublished diary on Syms Covington held at the Mitchell Library in Sydney, Australia. So he grounds his initial ideas for *Mr. Darwin's Shooter* on documented events and characters. However, he begins his process of converting factual records into fiction with the idea that sometimes "the historical record invites rather than unfolds an interpretation" (p. 2).

In his efforts to learn more about Covington's thinking during the voyage of the Beagle, McDonald researched Covington's archives and found them wanting. What is interesting about the Covington archives is that we find roughly eighty-five crew members that were involved in the entire expedition between 1831 and 1836. However, it seems that Covington's acquired skills and contributions to Darwin's important work is what informed McDonald's main focus in the book. He writes:

> I filled myself with seafaring lore and combed through Darwin's letters and diaries catching hold of clues. Covington learned collecting, preserving, shooting and packing skills from Darwin, slitting open bird stomachs,' poking through half digested contents, digging bones of prehistoric from Patagonia river banks, hefting, carting, sorting, storing. (p. 2).

Based on the forgoing description, McDonald discovered that Covington learned and accomplished the physical work of an apprenticed archeologist while Darwin accomplished the key work of interpreting the classified materials, usually undertaken by a zoologist and botanist.

McDonald states that letters that Darwin wrote to Covington later in life also provided useful clues whereby he could work backward. These letters can be characterized as condescending in tone, between "a distant master to a solid old servant"; Darwin congratulates the latter's material and family success in later life while continuing to request that Covington collect and send barnacles from nearby rocks (p. 5). McDonald states that "I based my story on such slender threads, perhaps, but I wanted more from this relationship than was there on show" (p. 5). Writing from a contemporary time and place, McDonald desires to discern a more egalitarian relationship between Darwin and Covington in the letters, in fact, a kind of love expressed by Darwin for Covington. This would not be so in the end.

IMAGINATION

In a journal article titled *Evolution of a Novel: Mr. Darwin's Shooter,* McDonald writes that Darwin's basic description of the process of evolution involves "numerous, successive, and slight modifications" of certain species like bird finches; McDonald says, "The same can be said of the writing process, as detail adapts to the needs of the story" (p. 1).[69] One of the needs was McDonald's desire to satisfy a longing for a kind of reconciliation of opposites as in the case involving Darwin and his "servant" Syms Covington, ultimately in my opinion, both allegorical symbols representing science and religion respectively.

McDonald wonders why Darwin does not like Covington and even describes him as an "odd sort of person" without providing any explanation as to why (p. 2). Herein seems to lie the key question to answer in McDonald's early writing process, arguing that "fiction comes out of just this vacuum of explanation, charting a relationship whose inner life begs to be *imagined*" (italics mine). McDonald uses the word *imagined* for what we might call grounded artistic license. However, McDonald writes that as he converted facts into fiction, he did not invent any of the "facts

---

[69] McDonald, R. Evolution of a Novel: *Mr. Darwin's Shooter. Australian Humanities Review,* pp. 1-6. Journal of Syms Covington. University of Oxford, Arts and Humanities Community Resource. Web. 4 April 2014. (http://arch.oucs.ox.ac.uk/detail/90994/index.html).

around the Darwin archive"; he simply "interpreted Covington for fictional purposes by taking the known facts of his life into the realm of speculation" (p. 4).

FICTIONAL TECHNIQUES

In this same article, McDonald argues that after having turned to novel writing, he discovered that using fictional techniques can actually help in grasping "the essence of an experience" and, in this case, Covington's relationship to Darwin and the former's underreported role and contributions to the earth-shaking work of the *Theory of Evolution*. In particular, McDonald wondered about Covington's psychological sense of self and subsequently created a Paul Bunyan Christian character "imbued with trusting faith from childhood, coming from an older England, a stranger to the ruling Anglicanism of the ruling order" (p. 4). He writes that Covington "heard his pa say that his boy would one day rise and stand equal to the Quentin House in money and fame . . . Those Quentins were Established Church and looked down on Baptists and Congregationalists." [70] As such, Covington's sense of self was clearly informed by the stark differences inherent in the English class system; Darwin did in fact belong to a wealthy Unitarian family but baptized in the Church of England.

FORMATIVE IMAGINATION AND FEELINGS

Be that as it may, McDonald also uses an advanced form of imagination to make his fictional novel work. He writes, "involved in the writing process, for me, is something closely related to formative imagery—a kind of abstraction hovering just ahead of me . . . It is like a pre-apprehended form, an image of where the

---

[70]   McDonald, R. *Mr Darwin's shooter*. London: Anchor, 1998, p. 15. Print.

novel's growth has to go before it will stop" a sort of "morphology" (p. 4). McDonald writes:

> Beforehand, with a novel, I have what might be roughly described as a subject area (war, flight, horses, water divining, fire, evolution) but no idea where I will go in terms of character, incident, and detail, except that thrown far ahead of me is the feeling I have to reach and satisfy.[71]

He writes that his writing style is, in a sense, closed-ended as it relates to where the story must not exceed; but to create the incidents or details of the new subject matter requires his imagination to fulfill the entire story. His writing objective is predetermined but not the details or contents of the story. When he *feels* the story is complete, then he stops.

SPECULATION

McDonald also asserts that a book contains a "pre-existing soul" manifesting shapes and colors that writers must bring up or, as in the Socratic sense, drawing out answers and responses from the soul using, in some cases, hypothetical questions or speculation. Ralph W. Emerson would describe education as a process of "drawing out the soul"; and so, it seems that what McDonald may be engaging in is an educational process, whereby he is drawing out more of the preexisting soul contained in nonfiction accounts, and, as a consequence, created a new fictional account containing different and but related colors and shapes. New insights and knowledge can therefore be produced for learning and change.

---

[71] McDonald, R. Evolution of a Novel: *Mr. Darwin's Shooter. Australian Humanities Review, p. 5.* Journal of Syms Covington. University of Oxford, Arts and Humanities Community Resource. Web. 4 April 2014. (http://arch.oucs.ox.ac.uk/detail/90994/index.html).

FINDINGS

Mr. Darwin's Shooter is a very good example of a writer borrowing from an important nonfictional event, the scientific work of Charles Darwin on the H.M.S. *Beagle,* to create a work of fiction that contains potentially many ideas and messages for the reader. McDonald, it seems to me, wove this kind of allegory using intellectual and affective tools. His research methods began with analyzing primary and secondary source materials. He did not simply restrict himself to the historical accounts' story but through reader-response approaches, decided to interpret for himself what might've been; he writes, "Luckily fiction is able to do that, and go where history cannot tread" (p. 6). But it was using his imagination and personal feelings that made it work so effectively.

What does the book mean to me? It seems to me that *Mr. Darwin's Shooter,* as a deeper intellectual work, serves as an allegorical tale wherein the story about the shift in influence and power from religion to science, represented by Covington and Darwin respectively, takes place. McDonald desires a reconciliation between both, but this would not be possible as of yet. The nineteenth century was the time when natural philosophy would achieve its independence from the enterprise of Christian theology; indeed, natural philosophy (science) would no longer serve as the handmaiden of theology moving forward in the modern and postmodern eras; this was important for major scientific and social breakthroughs which also have benefitted religions of all sorts. We can assume that the primacy of science within the postmodern Western world continues in its linear way of reasoning, as in the scientific method. But in the book entitled *The Zen Teachings of Master Lin-Chi,* we find that in Eastern civilization, gaining knowledge about our worlds actually requires that we search not the natural environment outside of us but within ourselves.

NON-WESTERN LITERARY IDEAS

In order to begin to understand *The Zen Teachings of Master Lin-Chi,* I started my thinking using linear theory in hopes of understanding Master Lin-Chi's very nonlinear concepts. As I read Chapter 11 of this book, I recalled how familiar his ideas were to a social learning theory advanced by Julian B. Rotter (1916-2014), a former professor of psychology at the Ohio State University. Rotter's social learning theory is what we currently understand as the *Locus of Control* (LOC).

Simply stated, the LOC theory suggests that individuals experience either internal or external locus of control; individuals who believe their own thinking and actions determine their fates have internal LOC, but those who believe their fates are at the mercy of external forces have external LOC. Thus, the latter type of believer fail to make the kind of progress in life that may bring more fulfillment. Master Lin-Chi would probably agree with the general idea of the LOC, but what is he doing and what does he want me to know through his teaching in Chapter 11? I assert that Master Lin-Chi uses metaphor, similes, and relevant quotations to teach the idea that only by trusting in and knowing themselves, and using their own faculties, can his students achieve true enlightenment.

SEARCHING INWARD VERSUS OUTWARD

Master Lin-chi argues that his students, or followers of the Way, fail to make progress in learning and life because "they don't have faith in themselves."[72] Indeed, he believes that one of the bad consequences of not having faith in themselves is that they engage their minds in a futile search for answers only in the external

---

[72] *"The Zen Teachings of Master Lin-Chi."* Translated by Watson Burton. New York: Columbia University Press, 1999, p. 23. Print.

environment and are thus tossed to and fro in life. Master Lin-chi writes, "But even if they get something, all it will be is words and phrases, pretty appearances. They'll never get at the living thought of the patriarchs" (p. 23).

The patriarchs and Buddhas were those individuals who disciplined their minds not to wander in the external environment for all their answers but instead realized that they didn't have any lack in the six faculties that included taste, sight, touch, hearing, smell, and intellect. Master Lin-Chi argues that by realizing that the light of the six faculties never goes out, "then you'd be the kind of person who has nothing to do for the rest of his life,"[73] meaning that this person, therefore, has no need to seek for anything outside of themselves.

Master Lin-Chi also differentiates between the lasting light of the six faculties and flickering lights, the latter representing the body and land of the Dharma way. He argues that followers of the Way can manipulate these flickering lights, bodily passions and material realm, and serve as the source of the Buddhas. Indeed, neither the body's organs nor the material spaces in the external world can teach or listen about the Dharma, the law of Buddhist teachings.

Master Lin-Chi deepens his argument by asserting that the mind transcends and actually works through the six faculties. He writes, "because this single mind has no fixed form, it is everywhere in a state of emancipation."[74] The single mind, interacting with the six faculties, is in a state of independence, essentially, not dependent on the external environment for enlightenment. But quoting from Li T'ung-hsuan's *Hsin Hua-yen-ching lu*, he also argues that "when feelings arise, wisdom is blocked; when thoughts waver, reality departs" (p. 25). Lin-Chi seems to suggest that followers of the Way guard against the emotional interferences to wisdom and lack of mental focus.

---

[73] Ibid., p. 24.
[74] Ibid., pp. 25-26.

Master Lin-Chi ultimately recommends that students of the Way not focus their minds on seeking Buddhahood but to be themselves. He writes, "You should stop and take a good look at yourselves . . . act ordinary, don't affect some special manner."[75] Echoes of the Oracle of Delphi's *Know Thyself* maxim seems appropriate here.

FINDINGS

What is Lin-Chi doing in Chapter 11? I believe he is using metaphor, similes, and relevant quotes to expound upon his central teaching points. He uses metaphors like body, flickering lights, light, and similes when he writes "like a burning house" for instance (p. 24). What does Master Lin-Chi want me to know through his teaching in Chapter 11? First of all, as a student, I must have faith in myself in the fact that I also carry the six faculties that my mind works with and through to achieve enlightenment. Moreover, failing to use the six faculties to take a good look at myself will prevent me from knowing my true self and put me in a frivolous search in the outside environment for all of my answers.

LITERATURE AND SOCIETY

The desire to *know*, or know better, about ourselves and the world around us is as old as the early stages of Homo sapiens' consciousness. It has been said by many that ignorance is the greatest of human evils. We can see the logic of this idea as when an illiterate person in any part of the world finds that, as a result of his or her inability to read, count, or communicate effectively, such individuals will resort to lying, stealing, or violence to get their basic human needs fulfilled. Ignorance, or the lack of background knowledge, of a neighbor near and far tends to produce fear of the

---

[75] Ibid., pp. 26-27.

unknown quite often leading to hate if not war between seemingly different communities. Literacy and understanding the "other" through important world literature can contribute to the lessening of suspicion or violence.

Improving our ability to read, apply quantitative skills, and communicate more effectively certainly has the potential for enhancing ethical behavior on the part of the individual, but we also see that human confidence as persons tends to increase when the fear and mystery involved in navigating strange environments decreases as a result of *knowing better*. Knowing better and more about what dimensions impinge on our thinking and lives increases personal awareness but also buy-in about participating and influencing the world around us as citizens.

We begin the next chapter with a discussion on two key concepts of learning, their ancient and contemporary conceptions, and their relationship to current educational processes. Educational processes ultimately produce various forms of learning and development—namely change—among students of all ages and throughout the ages.

CHAPTER 4

LEARNING AND THE EDUCATED PERSON: A CHANGE PROCESS

"Learning without thought is labor lost;
thought without learning is perilous."

Confucius

As we discussed in chapter one, the enterprise of philosophy initiated the opportunity to search for truth; engender, if not foster, a love for wisdom; and engage in a certain way of life. It was through philosophy-informed liberal learning approaches, which involved questions, dialogue, and discussion, that would enable the free individual to create lasting change in their lives. Credible and appropriate learning can produce the positive change necessary at the personal, social, and technological levels.

Embarking upon a meaningful discussion about what learning can be is a deep and never-ending intellectual journey as it has many differing conceptions when we consider time, place, and culture. The ancient Greeks initiated liberal learning institutions offering curricula designed to liberate the individual from the evils of ignorance, abuse of power, and ill-examined cultural assumptions. The idea of producing productive learning experiences was also true for Greek contemporaries in East Asia.

As quoted above, Confucius's (551-479 BCE) basic philosophy of *learning* involves *intentional thinking*, and if the latter is not involved in producing the former, then the individual is simply wasting their time. Indeed, according to Confucius, unfortunate consequences also can be experienced, personally and in society, when we engage in the thought processes that do not produce the necessary answers and change in our environments; in the worst-case scenario, an individual or group exhibits what Einstein defined as insanity, namely doing the same thing over and over again and actually expecting different results. The fruits of purposeful thinking, then, should produce meaningful and positive *change* in our minds and in the environments we operate in.

Socrates (469-399 BCE) posited a radically different philosophy of learning but explains this process as both an internal and external experience. While Confucius links learning with engaged and purposeful thinking to achieve what we call transfer of learning, Socrates's dialogue with the aristocratic Meno places the immortal human soul and its relationship to the cosmos at the center of learning. In Plato's dialogue titled *Meno,* Socrates uses the ideas of some of Athens' divine poets to explain his concept of learning saying:

> As the soul is immortal, has been born often, and has seen all things here and in the underworld, there is nothing which it has not learned: so it is in no way surprising that it can recollect the things it knew before, both about virtue and other things. As the whole of nature is akin, and the soul has learned everything, nothing prevents a man, after recalling one thing only—a process men call learning—discovering everything for himself, if he is brave and does not tire

of the search, for searching and learning are, as a whole, recollection.[76]

Socrates defines learning as a process involving both remembering at least one thing from the soul's memory banks, these representing a knowledge management systems of sorts, and engaging in search efforts or what we understand today as social or scientific inquiry; this should enable him or her in eventually "discovering everything."

The first part of his idea seems to us as counterintuitive as we generally understand learning to be only something we acquire from an external authority or experience in the environment, and this he seems to affirm. Moreover, some may associate Socrates's initial words about the soul having "been born often" to the metaphysical implications of reincarnation, but the emphasis he makes in the forgoing passage above relates more to *a priori* knowledge, that is, knowledge acquired beforehand through transcendent time or knowledge we're born with (for example, one plus four equals five); conversely, *a posteri* knowledge is acquired through experience with the material world around us as Aristotle would posit. Plato would, generally, subscribe to the former idea to inform his thinking about idealism.

How does one, therefore, access this tacit knowledge supposedly resident in the human soul? Socrates believed that by examining or by posing key questions relating to an issue being explored, an individual, slave or free, could recollect, or draw out, answers that were stored in the human soul.

But the soul's prior knowing could have limits as Meno's slave admitted to Socrates during his examination pertaining to knowledge of geometric figures. Indeed, acknowledging the lack of omniscience was not a common Athenian trait during this historical timeframe. The attitude of acknowledging his lack of

---

[76] *Meno. In Plato Five Dialogues: Euthyphro, Apology, Crito, Meno, Phaedo* (2nd ed.). Translated by G.M.A. Grube. Hackett Publishing Company. Indianapolis, IN, p. 71, 81D.

personal omniscience is what ultimately garnered Socrates the recognition from the *Oracle of Delphi* as the wisest man in Athens and much to the dismay of his know-it-all enemies who refused to do the same. Socrates states that further inquiry or searching on the part of the individual could potentially fill in the gaps of knowledge, if not create new light. Thus, in our contemporary social and scientific thinking, it is important to be committed to intellectual perseverance as many answers to the most complex questions in life often reveal themselves over time.

It is nonetheless difficult many times to admit our lack of omniscience as we know that others may judge us to be weak or unfit to exert certain influences, or leadership authority, in family, occupational, and other social contexts. We are told through morality teachings that intellectual humility is a virtue, but when faced with high-stake dilemmas, declarations of even ill-informed rhetoric seems to be the only option for the leader seeking to preserve any semblance of legitimacy in the real world. Thus, educational processes that encourage and develop the traits of intellectual humility on the part of learners and teachers alike are ideal. Socrates demonstrated or pretended intellectual humility and actually proved that a credible educational process could be experienced anywhere in the community.

PROFESSOR SOCRATES

While Socrates claimed that he did not teach anyone anything, as he did not charge fees to his listeners, his method of dialogue within the city streets of Athens certainly demonstrated that genuine constructivist learning could occur anywhere and anytime. Socrates's dialogical methods, an educational process the authorities labeled as human corruption, while threatening to the elites of Athens, would empower the average citizen and young persons to think for themselves. He believed his service to the gods was to serve as the gadfly of Athens wherein he would create the necessary cognitive dissonance in the minds of many arrogant and know-it-all Athenians.

By showing adults and the young alike how to question their own often faulty assumptions or an authority's version of truth, many important life issues could be explored and potentially resolved without the constant undue and flawed influence of external authorities. Socrates's dialogical methods would also serve as an antidote to the Sophists less than ideal curricular influences on the youth of Athens wherein negative forms of rhetorical skill were developed to substitute for genuine forms of social and democratic political rhetoric.

Socrates initiated thinking and examination of elite dogma and hegemonic assumptions by employing the first tool of the philosopher: the *question*. Questions such as what is justice, what is truth, what is courage, or how could we know for sure that many gods actually existed in the cosmos were explored or debated in the Athenian agora and alleyways. In addition to responding to the Sophists' negative influences in the city-state of Athens, Socrates questioned the elite and priestly class's monopoly on the nature of man's spiritual reality; in particular, humans' relationship, according to Homer, to supposed arbitrary and capricious gods who would engage in acts of both good and evil. This line of questioning could lead to more unsettling questions, such as is the priestly class achieving spiritual and political control over free human beings through superstitious tales.

DIALOGUE: AN EDUCATIONAL PROCESS

Suddenly, the idea of engaging in an educational process involving dialogue between citizen-peers gave voice and the experience of democracy to the average free Athenian; but this emerging intellectual environment required the tools of reason in order to appropriately question or accept the prevailing common and elite dogmas. For instance, citizens were empowered through Socrates's educational methods, which involved probing questions, the defining of terms, and particular follow-up questions, to construct for themselves how justice, courage, or true friendship could be manifested in the social and political context.

In one particular Platonic dialogue, Socrates would ask Polemarchus, "Is it just that we should do good *only* to our friends and evil to our enemies?" In fact, Socrates asks, why should any just person do any evil at all, even toward his enemies? Injuring another human deteriorates the integrity or qualities that make such a human good or potentially better. Certainly, Socrates is not suggesting that justice not be meted out when the law is broken as applying justice often involves visiting forms of incarceration or ostracization on the guilty person. The Socratic educational method tended to create the opportunity to challenge old assumptions, expose weak thinking, and produce higher and deeper levels of understanding for Athenians willing to engage in dialogue. Thus, we see the early forms of liberal learning experiences among free citizens. But how do Confucian and Socratic conceptions of learning relate to, and complement, what we currently know as the liberal educational process?

THE LIBERAL EDUCATIONAL PROCESS

Education as a term has its Latin roots in the word *educare,* which basically means to bring out or draw out from the individual. This can certainly mean just about anything a question draws out from a person's knowledge base, experience, or intuition relating to a certain matter being discussed. Emerson described the educational experience in a Socratic sense by characterizing it as a process of "drawing out the soul."[77] Thus, a genuine educational process, which should change an individual's perspective or way of living, is synonymous with the Socratic conception of *learning,* meaning, among other things, the unending process of recollecting,

---

[77] Mather, Cotton. *Christ the Fountaine of Life*, Ralph W. Emerson, journal entry, September 13, 1831, in Porte, p. 80.

dialoguing, applying new understanding, and, in many cases, documenting pertinent new understanding. Within the social context, this can certainly include others' insights, thinking, or perspectives, especially when attempting to solve organizational challenges. Ideally, the process and experience of engaging in respectful dialogue about important ideas and organizational matters among a group of peers begins within the academic context. This was Plato's idea when he established the Academy, and this is true of many of our institutions of liberal learning today.

Reviewing a few educational approaches taken by certain liberal arts programs is instructive at this point. In Columbia University's *Core Curriculum* program, we see that students share a common educational experience. The university states:

> The Core Curriculum is the set of common courses required of all undergraduates and considered the necessary general education for students, irrespective of their choice in major. The communal learning—with all students encountering the same texts and issues at the same time—and the critical dialogue experienced in small seminars are the distinctive features of the Core.[78]

Thus, the communal learning approach is emphasized at Columbia University wherein students dialogue critically amongst themselves and the faculty member about a set of common books. The communal learning approach is often at the heart an institution's mission, again, wherein students are required to dialogue and defend their ideas and impressions of a book passage or poem. For instance, at St. John's College, located in Santa Fe, New Mexico, and Annapolis, Maryland, the *Seminar* is central to its liberal learning model:

---

[78] "The Core Curriculum." Columbia University. Web. 4 April 2014.

Often described as the heart of the St. John's program, the seminar is central to the life of the college. Co-led by two tutors, seminar classes have 18 to 20 students . . . Seminars begin with a question meant to invite and provoke inquisitive conversation that may continue long after the two-hour period is over. The seminar draws on the students' wonder, attentiveness, judgment, imagination, openness to new ideas, willingness to be refuted, patience, courage, collegiality, leadership, and general resourcefulness. Seminar is intended to develop attentive reading habits, elicit clarity of thought and generosity of spirit, and encourage a willingness to embrace unfamiliar territory. As the part of the Program in which students most take responsibility for their own learning, seminar embodies the college's mission in its purest form.[79]

This model of learning is initiated through a tutor's question that invites and provokes inquisitive conversation that many times continues outside of the classroom. Students' cognitive and affective traits are drawn upon to liven and enlighten the conversation in class. At Saint Mary's College of California, the *Collegiate Seminar* offers an educational experience where:

A small group of students and a professor sit around a table and talk about books. They argue; they theorize; they question. They examine passages closely and connect them to other passages, other books, other experiences. They talk about ideas as living things.[80]

The *Collegiate Seminar* at Saint Mary's does not necessarily focus on a "great books" curricula; it does make room for dialogue

---

[79] "The Seminar." St. John's College. Web. 22 April 2014.
[80] "Collegiate Seminar." Saint Mary's College of California. Web. 22 April 2014.

about books and literature that may not be considered part of the "western" canon but are nonetheless important to the global commons discussion.

The initial stages of an effective educational process also heeds Confucius's warnings against "learning without thought," meaning that we must engage in what in critical thinking is called *metacognition,* simply described as thinking about our thinking. For instance, as I write my essay which I intend to deliver before an audience, I should ask myself: Will some of the terms I am using need to be defined for those without background knowledge of my ideas? Or perhaps: Should I provide one or two examples of what I mean in the dialogue?

Genuine educational processes involve, again, applying previous knowledge when relevant, keeping an open mind, questioning the assumptions that underpin previous understanding or knowledge, and discussing what implications may apply to an issue, especially in light of new data or information. Knowledge embedded in ours or others' souls, or a document, may no longer be true or relevant to a current situation. Thus, we include the standard of accepting the answer which explains the most available data, and this requires learning *with* thought and not always accepting what we currently think we know without question. It seems, then, that Confucian and Socratic learning places an emphasis on metacognition, *a priori* knowledge, and continuing research; however, the contemporary understanding of learning places more emphasis on the Aristotelian idea of external stimuli, or experience, and less on Plato's emphasis on internal ideas.

In the contemporary empirically based world, the Confucian, Socratic, and Aristotelian conceptions of learning are being applied both in the world of ideas and experience. Learning can be currently defined as "the acquisition of knowledge or skills through study, experience, or being taught,"[81] or the "modification of a behavioral tendency by experience,"[82] and "the process of gaining

---

[81] "Learning." Oxford Dictionaries. Web. 22 April 2014.
[82] "Learning." Merriam-Webster Dictionary. Web. 22 April 2014.

information through observation."[83] From the forgoing formal definitions of what learning can be understood to be, we see that it involves the acquisition of knowledge, a change or modification of certain behaviors based on particular external experiences, or a formal process designed to help us test an hypothesis or confirm new data through a seemingly objective epistemological process we currently call the scientific method. Most new learning, however, requires the help of a guide or teacher employing methods that increase the transfer of learning.

ART AND SCIENCE OF TEACHING

The ancient Sophists were known for their teaching skills as teachers of rhetoric and dialectics. Quite often, these Sophists used their teaching skills to develop in others the ability to manipulate the use of words and language as they employed political rhetoric. We can certainly agree that the Sophists were very good at employing their teaching skills to teach others how to obfuscate knowledge but not for creating greater transparency and trust in society.

Comprehensive educational processes involve teaching methods, simply understood to be methods of conveying, affirming, and confirming to an audience data, information, or knowledge that is relevant to learning objectives. I have often said to new faculty members that "telling is not teaching." Effective teaching involves the right content knowledge and an appropriate delivery style. The approaches used by a teacher vary between those used with children, college students, or adult learners, but teaching is basically understood as "the process by which individuals are

---

[83]   Schulte, Oliver. Formal Learning Theory. *The Stanford Encyclopedia of Philosophy (Summer 2012 Edition)*. Ed. Edward N. Zalta. Web. 22 April 2014.

introduced to a culture by more skilled members," presumably of a discipline or profession.[84]

More skilled members in this sense means that a teacher is viewed as a subject matter expert or must have the experience or formal credentials which prove to society that he or she offers a valid knowledge base that can inform and produce positive change in others. Certainly, the more effective teacher is an individual who continues to learn more about their discipline, and this sometimes occurs through the insights of his or her students. But what methods does a teacher use to initiate new members into a new culture or knowledge domain?

Formal definitions of what "teaching" can be understood to be yield vague or circular descriptions that only address something that, for instance, a teacher or professor does. We need to instead refer to a synonym of teaching, namely the term *instruction,* to begin to better understand what this important communication skill actually is. Merriam-Webster (2013) online simply defines *instruction* as "a statement that describes how to do something." Presumably, the "statement" can be either verbal or written. The essence of teaching, then, seems to involve a process wherein an instructor uses statements intended to inform someone in how to understand a concept or do something. A subdefinition of instruction is described as "an outline or manual of technical procedure." Assuming that a new or seasoned faculty member can inform others simply because they hold the requisite graduate-level degree or professional experience does not guarantee that such a person can teach effectively. Oftentimes, new faculty members will teach in the style of their favorite professor or teacher. This isn't necessarily the best approach to developing teaching skills; thus, we see within many colleges and universities the establishment of new faculty development programs.

---

[84] Driver, R., Asoko, H., Leach, J., Mortimer, E. and Scott, P. Constructing scientific knowledge in the classroom. *Educational Researcher, 23*(7), 1994, p.7. Print.

One of the earliest faculty development programs was found in the *Jesuit Ratio Studorium of 1599*, the first formal faculty development document written to help schools and college teachers in the burgeoning Jesuit education system in Spain, Italy, Portugal, Austria, Bohemia, and France. At the time of his death, the founder of the Society of Jesus, Ignatius Lopez of Loyola (1491-1556) had founded thirty-three schools, including the Roman College in Rome, Italy. According to Farrall (1971), the *Jesuit Ratio Studorium* provided faculty development guidance to the professors of Sacred Scripture, Hebrew, Scholastic Theology, Cases of Conscience, Philosophy, Moral Philosophy, and Mathematics.

The various teaching methods that are manifested during the educational process include *lectures* where a unidirectional communication approach is taken by the instructor to impart knowledge or new pieces of information to an audience of any size; *guided discussion* or Socratic examination occurs when the instructor shifts from her lecture to ask or solicit questions from her students in order to achieve more clarity, precision, or confirmation about learning goals; *indirect teaching*, wherein the instructor engages in a discussion with a guest expert in front of students about a key issue or learning module being explored by the class itself; *team teaching*, where more than one instructor shares the load of a course to teach particular segments of a course, especially due to their specific subject matter expertise; and finally, *facilitation*, where the instructor suspends his authority as the teacher and, in turn, delegates the educational process to student groups in his class so as to create an opportunity for the learners to inform each other and to engage in analysis, synthesis, and evaluation of new insights.

Thus, the educational process involves drawing from students' insights and experiences, requiring that they critically analyze current assumptions underpinning what they think they know, and employing teaching and multidirectional instructional approaches that should produce new insights and change in students' lives.

THE PROFESSOR, DIALECTICS, AND HIGHER LEARNING

The adjective *higher* preceding the term *learning* usually suggests that most of the discussion on such a topic will address advanced forms of postsecondary education, training, or professional development. Defining higher learning can also be a challenge, but herein, it can be understood to be the educational process involving a curriculum encountered within an accredited college, university, or institute; instead of diplomas, undergraduate or graduate degrees are conferred upon those who have successfully completed a curriculum requiring mastery of coursework in general education, electives, a minor, a major, often experiential learning, and a master's thesis, or a doctoral dissertation in the case of graduate school. Higher learning can occur as well at the informal level. Service learning models, experiential learning approaches, community centered debates, a museum tour, a book club, prison education programs, or a lecture offered through a faith-based or service organization can be examples of informal learning opportunities that do not all necessarily afford transferable academic credit but can nonetheless produce change in mind, body, or spirit.

Far from being a unidirectional process, purposeful higher learning experienced within an educational context enables teachers and learners to participate in a Socratic discovery process by including, if not requiring, learners' insights during study or concrete dialogical experiences. The Socratic educational method has often been described as a midwifing process in that, through the use of key questions, teachers and professors can help students recollect or trigger the birthing of new insights or knowledge that resides within an individual's soul or mind. Thus, a higher learning experience, as in philosophy, involves searches for clarification, new understanding, or truth wherein, through a guided dialectical process involving genuine participation of a teacher and more than one individual, new change or inconclusive learning can be realized for that moment or in perpetuity. The following section is based on an article the author published in 2008 within the *Online Journal of Workforce Education and Development,* Southern Illinois University Carbondale, Volume III, Issue 1—Spring 2008, which is particularly centered on adult learners engagement with a liberal learning process.[85]

ADULT LEARNERS AND THE DIALECTICAL PROCESS

As a consequence of globalization, continuous technological innovation, and demographic population shifts occurring internationally,[86] the early twenty-first-century adult learner must expect to be more committed to what is now termed as "lifelong learning"; this presumably to remain viable in a world increasingly requiring cross cultural competence and more frequent updating of our knowledge, skills, and attitudes (KSA). Adult learners, particularly in the developed world, are especially concerned about this new and accelerating global phenomenon, given that they are increasingly competing with a global talent pool.[87] Indeed, accessibility and affordability of education, training and development opportunities for adult learners is one of the most critical issues affecting social and economic stability in contemporary societies.[88]

Accessibility and affordability of relevant training and higher education opportunities certainly are not the main challenges encountered by adult learners. Adult learners, once enrolled in

[85] Chaves, Christopher A. Adult Learners and The Dialectical Process: A Validating Constructivist Approach To Learning Transfer And Application. Online Journal of Workforce Education and Development Volume III, Issue 1—Spring 2008. Web. 22 April 2014.

[86] Karoly, L.A. and Panis, C.A. *The 21ᵗ century at work: Forces shaping the future workforce and workplace in the United States.* Santa Monica, CA: RAND Corporation, 2004. Print.

[87] Florida, Richard. *The flight of the creative class: The new global competition for talent.* New York: Harper Collins Publishers, 2006. Print.

[88] Merriam, S. A. and Caffarella, R. S. *Learning in adulthood: A comprehensive guide.* San Francisco: Jossey-Bass Publishers, 1999. Print.

liberal arts education or career and technical training programs, face a myriad of challenges as they attempt to assimilate new KSAs required in twenty-first-century social and occupational settings. For instance, whether encountered at a community college, in a degree completion program offered through a four-year liberal arts college, or a traditional university program setting, adult students often engage their education within curricular forms and content that are still largely tailored more for traditional-age students. Far too often, the instructional strategies used with adult students are informed largely by a "pedagogical" teaching paradigm, often defined as the art and science of teaching children. The student, regardless of age, it is assumed is lacking in pertinent knowledge and remains passive while the instructor dispenses a monologue about the subject matter at hand. This often leads to instructor frustration, in that, lecture content delivery does not necessarily achieve crucial transfer of learning, [89]much less personal transformation.

Conversely, "andragogical" curricular methods, characterized as the art and science of teaching adults,[90] informs yet a different teaching and learning paradigm, one where students' needs, knowledge and experience largely dictate what the form and content of the curriculum will offer; the instructor is simply a "facilitator" attempting to achieve, not necessarily professional parity with his or her students, but an egalitarian relationship with students regarding learning objectives;[91] ultimately, adult students are to be self-directed learners.

---

[89] Lang, J. M. Beyond lecturing. *The Chronicle of Higher Education,* 53(6), 2006. Web. (http://chronicle.com.proxy.lib.siu.edu/weekly/v53/i06/06c00101.htm).

[90] Knowles, M. *The modern practice of adult education: Andragogy versus pedagogy.* New York: Cambridge Books, 1970. Print.

[91] Howell, C.L. *Facilitating responsibility for learning in adult community college students.* Los Angeles: University of California, Los Angeles, ERIC Clearinghouse for Community Colleges, 2001. (ERIC Document Reproduction Service No. ED 451 841).

Emerging adult learning theory has also been informed by Kolb's experiential learning constructs.[92] Not only must adult students' knowledge and experience be brought into the classroom discourse, but it is within for instance, real world case-study assignments in the classroom, where exchange between students and their instructors generate new understanding as a consequence of their experiences together. Indeed, Knowles asserts that the curriculum must create a classroom attitude of mutuality between teachers and students as joint investigators. But what form of curricular structure lends itself to an organized exchange of experience, knowledge, and ideas likely to bring about a better transfer of learning among adult students?

This article will argue that, centered within the constructivist tradition, by applying a dialectical curricular framework (thesis, antithesis, synthesis), adult educators can achieve relevant transfer of learning, indeed meaningful transformation, among adult students. This framework can facilitate the exchange between old and new understandings, challenge and/or affirm existing paradigms, and create new knowledge and application to students' personal and occupational lives.

In addition, the argument is also made that crucial to this learning process is that the instructor assume the role of, not the sage on the stage, but a subject matter expert by incorporating adult-appropriate pedagogical teaching strategies, when addressing foundational content knowledge, at critical junctures during the course. According to Cross (1981), should an educator seek to know how to help a student learn, in general "he needs to know how teachers should behave in order to facilitate learning." [93] In particular, according to Lang, students "need a strong factual and conceptual foundation in order to work effectively in groups or hold intelligent discussions or solve problems." [94] In essence, the

---

[92] Kolb, D. *Experiential learning: Experience as the source for learning and development.* New Jersey: Prentice Hall, 1984. Print.

[93] Cross, K.P. *Adults as learners: Increasing participation and facilitating learning.* San Francisco: Jossey-Bass, 1981. Print.

[94] Ibid. p. 2.

instructor must be viewed as an expert in their field, not simply a facilitator of divergent views, to establish and maintain the credibility required of leaders. Indeed, the point is often made when recruiting adult students to various degree programs that the faculty offer, not only academic credentials, but "real-world" experience that enhance the learning objectives.

Certainly not a new concept but, instructors employ both adult-appropriate pedagogical and andragogical teaching methods (form), but apply a dialectical process to encourage and incorporate students' knowledge, ideas, and experiences into the curriculum (content) in an effort to create a heightened sense of commitment on the part of students, a richer and deeper classroom discourse, and improved transfer of learning. The Constructive Dialectical Curriculum Model conceptualizes this idea. The following literature review will begin with a brief treatment of foundational learning theories including behaviorism, constructivism, and the origins and purpose of Hegelian dialectics. Next, the review establishes the theoretical foundations of adult learning theorists including the works of Knowles (1984)[95] and Kolb (1984). Particular attention will also be given to transformational learning theory advanced by Mezirow (2000).[96] In the final section, each of the major theorists discussed are aligned to coalesce their contributions in support of the Constructive Dialectical Curriculum Model.

LITERATURE REVIEW

Before placing the three foundational theories within the context of adult learning theory, defining their basic meaning is necessary. Two major theories inform pedagogical and andragogical

---

[95] Kolb, D. *Experiential learning: Experience as the source for learning and development.* New Jersey: Prentice Hall, 1984. Print.

[96] Mezirow, J. *Learning to think like an adult: Core concepts of transformational theory.* In *Learning as transformation: Critical perspectives on a theory in progress.* San Francisco: Jossey-Bass, 2000. Print.

learning theory and practice: behaviorism and constructivism, the latter being a branch of cognitive theory. Behaviorists assert that learning can only be assessed through direct observation; positive and negative reinforcement feedback is necessary for learning and unlearning. Behaviorism seems more appropriate to understanding how younger students can learn (e.g., cognitive and affective learning) but may be applicable to adult learning objectives as in the case of psychomotor skills development (Cross, 1981). Behaviorism, then, is largely concerned about specific visible learning outcomes; constructivism, on the other hand, concerns itself with creating an environment where a learning process can proceed creatively and productively.

CONTRUCTIVISM FOR NEW UNDERSTANDING

Constructivism stems from cognitive learning theory, and it was cognitive psychologists who first rejected behaviorists' earlier claims about relying too much on overt individual behaviors to explain changes and learning, which was usually assumed to occur passively. Cognitive learning theorists instead argue that a thinking individual interprets "sensations and gives meaning to events that impinge upon his conscience."[97] Constructivism, therefore, is essentially "a search for meaning . . . Knowledge is not simply 'out there' to be attained; is it constructed by the learner."[98]

Merriam and Caffarella (1999) assert that "constructivists differ as to the nature of reality, the role of experience, what knowledge is of interest, and whether the process of meaning making is primarily individual or social" (p. 261). It is individual in the sense that meaning making is based on a student's "previous and

---

[97] Grippin, P. and Peters, S. *Learning theory and learning outcomes.* Lanham: University Press of America, 1984. Print.

[98] Baumgartner, L.M. (2003). Andragogy: A foundational theory/set of assumptions. *In Adult learning theory: A primer. Information Series No. 392.* Columbus: Center on Education and Training for Employment, College of Education, The Ohio State University, 2003, p. 2. Print.

current knowledge structure" (p. 261) and occurs independently. Social constructivism, on the other hand, occurs when "individuals engage socially in talk and activities about shared problems or tasks." Meaning-making is therefore a "dialogic process involving persons-in-conversations, and learning is seen as the process by which individuals are introduced to a culture by more skilled members" (Driver et al., 1994, p. 7), as in the case of subject matter experts. Constructivist dialogical processes often complement and inform dialectical epistemologies, and in particular, Hegel's dialectical framework can serve as a model.

THE HEGELIAN DIALECTIC

The term *dialectics* is used in many variations (e.g., Socratic dialectic, transcendental dialectic, dialectical materialism) but has its roots in Plato's dialectic method of cross-examination used in support of his philosophical positions; the Greek translation defines it simply as, the art of conversation. Georg Wilhelm Hegel (1770-1831) extended Plato's dialectics and created more of a discourse framework whereby a current *thesis* can be challenged by a contradiction or *antithesis*, with the resultant inherent tension tending to produce a *synthesis* on, usually, a complex multidimensional matter.

Merriam and Caffarella (1999) argue that what must become a part of adults' ways of thinking is dialectical information processing. Indeed, dialectical thinking "allows for the acceptance of alternative truths and ways of thinking . . ." (Merriam and Caffarella, 1999, p. 152). As such, the purpose of a dialectical approach to curriculum design is to create a validating mechanism framework wherein student-peers and their instructors engage in conversation or disputation within intentional, logical, and constructivist learning environments; this approach essentially serves as a learning blueprint about what students have to offer in the dialog, what unknown areas or contradictions they have yet to consider, and where they might arrive intellectually in the educational experience. New discoveries and knowledge bases are then recycled back into students' personal and occupational worlds. While constructivism can set forth one of the central philosophical foundations to adult learning methods, Hegel's dialectic provides a validating mechanism for discourse and debate.

Next, we explore how andragogy helps to explain many of the inherent variables necessary for individual constructivism and, second, how experiential learning theory can create an environment whereby social constructivism can occur among adult students. Understanding the basic psycho-social dimensions of adult students who are poised to learn is crucial; Knowles's work on andragogy can begin this process and seems to complement and inform a dialectical curricular structure.

KNOWLES'S ANDRAGOGY

The term *andragogy* was originally termed by German teacher Alexander Kapp in 1833 to explain Plato's idea that individuals continue learning into adulthood (Baumgartner, 2003). The term was used more widely in Europe before Malcolm Knowles popularized it in the United States beginning in the early 1960s. *Andragogy* is defined simply as "the art and science of helping adults learn" (Knowles, 1984, p. 43). This construct offers five assumptions about adult learners: (1) adult students must transition from dependent learning toward self-directed learning; (2) adults' greater reservoir of experience can be used as a learning tool; (3) adults' readiness to learn is based on actual social roles; (4) adults need to apply new knowledge and skills immediately (task-centered); and (5) adults are internally, versus externally, motivated about learning new things (Knowles, 1984, 1990).

Criticism has been lodged against andragogy, however, in that it was not quite clear if it stood for a theory of learning or teaching or if it qualified as a theory at all;[99] theories must have a credible level of predictability. St. Clair (2002) agrees that andragogy may not qualify as an adult learning theory because it fails to clarify "how and why people learn";[100] Knowles's assumptions 2 through 5 seem to refute this claim at some level however. Originally, Knowles (1970) argued that andragogy would essentially replace the need for pedagogical learning approaches. In the aftermath of some criticism, Knowles (1980) clarified his original claims by postulating that human development may actually occur along a continuum, from pedagogy to andragogy.

Cross (1981) disagrees arguing that this continuum does not truly exist since subject-centered learning and problem-centered learning tend to "appear more dichotomous in nature" (p. 225). Moreover, Delahaye, Limerick, and Hearn (1994) argue that students can fit in differing categories; they may be either low pedagogy/high andragogy or high pedagogy/low andragogy. Nonetheless, Merriam and Caffarella (1999) assert that, for practitioners who work with adult learners, andragogy can "be a helpful rubric for better understanding adults as learners" (p. 277/8), be viewed as a more humanistic approach addressing adult education, or, as Knowles (1989) cited, "as a basis for an emergent theory" (p. 112).[101] Yet while Knowles's (1984) work on andragogy provides a bases for beginning to understand *how* and *why* adult learners can experience a form of individual constructivism, David Kolb (1984) believed that new experiences could be created and used as a source for new learning and development among adult learners (social constructivism); this can be possible by recognizing

---

[99] Hartree, A. Malcolm Knowles' theory of andragogy: A critique. *International Journal of Lifelong Education, 3*(3), 1984, p. 203-210. Print.

[100] St. Clair, R. *Andragogy revisited: Theory for the 21ˢᵗ century? Myths and realities.* Columbus, OH: ERIC Clearinghouse on Adult, Career, and Vocational Education, The Ohio State University, 2002. (ERIC Document Reproduction Service No. ED468 612).

[101] Knowles, M. S. (1989). *The making of an adult educator: An autobiographical journey.* San Francisco: Jossey-Bass, 1989, p. 112. Print.

and leveraging the contributions of different learning styles experienced through different discourse options.

KOLB'S EXPERIENTIAL LEARNING CONSTRUCT

David Kolb's (1984) work on experiential learning can be associated to a dictum postulated by Confucius, "Tell me, and I will forget. Show me, and I may remember. Involve me, and I will understand."[102] Indeed, Kant (1788) begins his work entitled *Critique of Pure Reason* by asserting that all human knowledge stems from experience. Kolb (1984) defines experiential learning as "the process whereby knowledge is created through the transformation of experience" (p. 41). He further clarifies experiential learning encounters by asserting their constructivist nature, in that it is "a process, not an outcome; that learning is best facilitated when students apply their own beliefs and ideas to a topic" (Chaves, 2006).[103] Adult students' experiences, knowledge, ideas, and beliefs applied to practical activities, accomplished within a group or team-based context, often create opportunities for transformational experiences and the consequent new learning. Kolb's (1984) experiential learning theory offers four dialogical discourse learning stages whereby philosophical, ideological, theoretical, and practical subject matter issues can be discussed, debated, and assimilated where appropriate; each of the four discourse experiences can be considered learning styles, or strengths, resident among many but not all adult learners. They include concrete experiences, reflective observations, abstract conceptualization, and active experimentation.

Concrete experiences can include the analysis and discussion of article-based issues, textbook readings, lectures, guest lectures,

---

[102] "Experiential Learning." Web. 3 Mar 2008. (http://www.reviewing. co.uk/research/experientiallearning.htm#2).

[103] Chaves, C. A. Involvement, development, and retention: Theoretical foundations and potential extensions for adult community college students. *UCLA Community College Review, 34*(2), 2006, p. 149.

guided discussion experiences, and Internet-based learning; *reflective observations* can include group discussion, free-writing, and brainstorming exercises; *abstract conceptualization* involves self-direction and the freedom to hypothesize about subject matter; and, lastly, *active experimentation* involves the use of the case-study method concerning real-world examples for new learning and application. Indeed, these are the learning contexts whereby many students can engage "socially in talk and activities about shared problems or tasks" (Driver et al. 1994, p. 7).

While Kolb's (1984) work on using new experiences as a source of learning and development accords a four-stage constructivist learning approach, some criticism has also be lodged against his work. For instance, Forrest (2004) argues from a training perspective that there are a variety of processes which can occur all at once and that some of Kolb's learning stages can be left out completely.[104] Moreover, she states that the inventory was tested and developed within a Western-centric context, essentially leaving but non-Western cultural ontologies. Although, Chaves (2006) argues that Kolb's four-stage experiential learning model can apply within group-based cultures as adult learners have proven in some Southeast Asian contexts. Nonetheless, Rogers (1996),[105] while admitting that Kolb's experiential learning theory has refocused learning back onto the student, posits along with Miettinen (2000)[106] that the inventory's results are based solely on the way learners rated themselves and not in relation to other adult students in their learning environment, which serves to enhance reasoning and learning outcomes.

Ultimately, Kolb (1984) posits that "it is more effective to design curriculum so that there is some way for learners of every

---

[104] Forrest, C. *Kolb's learning cycle. Train the trainer, volume 12.* Ely, Cambridgeshire: Fenman Professional Training Resources, 2004. Print.

[105] Rogers, A. *Teaching Adults (2nd ed.).* Buckingham: Open University Press, 1996. Print.

[106] Miettinen, R. The concept of experiential learning and John Dewey's theory of reflective thought and action. *International Journal of Lifelong Education, 19*(1), 2000, pp. 54-72. Print.

learning style to engage with the topic. Curriculum design should follow the learning cycle of experiencing, reflecting, thinking and acting . . . an initial way to connect with the material and then begin to stretch his learning capability in other learning modes" (http://www.learningfromexperience.com/faq). Indeed, Cross (1981), citing Perry's (1970)[107] work on intellectual development in college, writes, "The role of the teacher (or facilitator) . . . is to help the individual advance to the next level of cognitive development through designing educational experiences that will challenge the learner to 'reach' for growth-enhancing cognitive experiences."[108]

Oftentimes, growth enhancing cognitive experiences actually engender productive personal and social transformation on the part of adults. Mezirow's (2000) model on transformative learning elevates the discussion from one based on the need and importance of transactional forms of learning processes over to one where the consequent personal transformation on the part of students can actually lead to wider, positive social transformation.

MEZIROW'S THEORY ON TRANSFORMATIVE LEARNING

Whereas Knowles's work on andragogy and Kolb's work on experiential learning enlightens the discussion about adult learner characteristics and learning styles and the accompanying discourse methods, respectively, Mezirow's (2000) work on transformative learning goes deeper into the cognitive and affective nature of understanding who is, as Georg Hegel described it, the "other." Mezirow's theory about transformative learning was predicated on Habermas's (1984)[109] communicative learning theory. Essentially, communicative learning theory asserts that understanding what an individual communicates goes beyond their spoken words.

---

[107] Perry, W. G. (1970). *Forms of intellectual and ethical development in the college years.* Austin: Holt, Rinehart & Winston, 1970, p. 231. Print.
[108]

[109] Habermas, J. *The theory of communicative action.* Boston: Beacon Press, 1984.

According to Mezirow (2000), what is also necessary to the constructivist meaning making process is understanding a speaker's feelings, intentions, and assumptions; this is when transformative learning can occur.

Although informed by Habermas, Mezirow's (2000) empirical work was primarily based on the experiences of women reentering higher education after having been out of a formal learning process for a time. Mezirow's (2000) model offers a ten-step ontological change process which emphasizes critical reflection and in "reflective discourse" (p. 11). Baumgartner (2003) describes the process as "talking with others—in order to arrive at a perspective transformation or change in world view," which can happen suddenly or in a gradual sense (p. 19).

The ten-step transformative process generally involves the following steps: an individual will experience (1) a disorienting dilemma; (2) followed by fear, guilt, shame, or anger; (3) subsequent critical reflection; (4) a reaching out to others undergoing similar experience(s); (5) the exploration of new relationships, roles, or courses of actions; (6) planning a particular course of action; (7) gaining the necessary knowledge, skills, or attitudes for implementing the chosen course of action; (8) implementation of a new role on a provisional bases; (9) realizing confidence in the new role; and (10) reintegration into life based on new conditions, informed especially by one's new perspectives. Baumgartner (2003) writes that, basically, transformative learning's main ingredients include experience, critical reflection, and reflective discourse; the latter enables individuals to "challenge each other's assumptions and building consensus" (p. 20).

Criticism has also been registered against Mezirow's (2000) work on transformative learning. Baumgartner (2003), drawing from Collard and Law's (1989) original questioning of Mezirow's epistemological assumptions, writes that Mezirow's work on transformational learning is incomplete simply because it's focus is centered only on the individual, to the exclusion of the socio-political context although some would argue that Mezirow (2000) is advocating for an individual constructivist form of experience.

Nonetheless, other critics argue that culture (e.g., race, class, and gender) and context are important variables to recognize as having an impact on the transformative learning process (Taylor, 1998).[110] Indeed, Caruth (2000),[111] citing the experiences of black men attending the Million Man March in Washington DC, posits that Mezirow's work does not address, in particular, racial group identity dynamics in the transformative learning process.

The foregoing literature review can thus serve to establish the philosophical, theoretical, and metaphysical aspects necessary for informing and constructing a valid curricular design appropriate to adult learners undergoing academic, occupational, and/or professional training. While a foregone conclusion, in humans' constant pursuit for new knowledge, updated skills, and attitudinal changes, it becomes quite obvious that adult learners carry more advantages concerning KSAs due to their personal and occupational experience levels. However, disadvantages or challenges also exist in that since older individuals are "more set in their ways," unlearning outdated knowledge, skills, attitudes, or expectations can pose a challenge to themselves and those teaching for and facilitating among adult students. As such, adult learners' ability to engage ontological contradictions may require a more intentional, multistage process whereby new ideas can be explored and assimilated at some level, especially with the aid of communal reflection.

So how can understanding Knowles's work on andragogy aid in the initiation of a dialectical process appropriate to adult students? Moreover, how can an experiential learning curricular model serve the purposes of a *dialectical antithesis* process which is designed

---

[110] Taylor, E. W. *The theory and practice of transformational learning: A critical review. Information series no. 374.* Columbus, OH: ERIC Clearinghouse on Adult, Career, and Vocational Education, The Ohio State University, 1998. (ERIC Document Reproduction Service No. ED423422).

[111] Caruth, D. *African American male transformative learning: An Afro-centric study of the Million Man March.* Unpublished doctoral dissertation, University of Wyoming, Laramie, 2000.

to amend or dislodge outdated KSAs with new understanding? Using a dialectical discourse model, can the necessary synthesis occur in the classroom and how? Does transformational learning occur within all students and, if not, why? As Driver et al. (1994) assert, at the core of constructivist instructional (curricular) approaches lie in operationalizing "practical activities supported by group discussions" (p. 6). It is in this epistemological context, in classroom, workplace, or virtual environments, wherein the student enters into community to achieve intellectual synergy and transformational changes related to their KSAs, which impact their social and occupational contexts.

If the Hegelian dialectical framework can serve as the overall validating mechanism recipe among students and their instructors, what specific curricular ingredients can we use in the classroom to bring about positive learning synthesis, indeed, positive personal transformation? To begin answering the foregoing questions, we next turn to a discussion on andragogy's relation to the dialectical thesis, the dialectical antithesis' relationship to experiential learning curricula, and its impact on transfer of learning for personal and socio-occupational transformation. However, we begin with a basic description of the Constructive Dialectical Curriculum Model, which serves to conceptualize the entire curricular concept.

A DIALECTIC MODEL'S IMPACT ON ANDRAGOGY, EXPERIENTIAL LEARNING, AND TRANSFORMATIONAL LEARNING

Specifically, the *Constructive Dialectical Curriculum Model* suggests that adults bring unique personal and occupational knowledge, skills, and attitudes (KSA) to the educational process. Once inside of a learning context, the adult learner engages in adult appropriate pedagogical and andragogical curricular exercises which draw out, affirm, and utilize their personal and occupational KSAs, leverage their readiness to learn new things, and enhance their motivation in order to launch new and often challenging ontological and learning paradigms.

Next, the instructor, or facilitating subject matter expert, helps the class to begin the transition from a thesis understanding (current paradigms) over to the antithetical learning position. He or she will use experiential learning curricular strategies to attempt to bring about a synthesis regarding the subject matter at hand. Even before synthesis has been reached, students have been able to begin to cycle new understanding back into their personal and occupational lives. However, it is only until complete synthesis has been achieved that students can cycle the best new understanding back into their personal and professional lives. This recursive learning process begins by recognizing some of the assumptions andragogy contributes to the initial stages of a dialectical learning process.

Andragogy and the Dialectical Thesis

If the Hegelian dialectic can provide a validating mechanism framework, or discourse framework, for a teaching and learning exchange among adult students, deploying most andragogy's assumptions about their knowledge and experience base is crucial. What is useful for our purposes is the acknowledgement that andragogy's assumptions 2, 3, and 5 inform the starting point, or *thesis,* of a dialectical adult learning model. Again, affirming and utilizing students' prior knowledge and experience as a learning resource (assumption #2) in the initial, and latter, stages of a dialectical discourse is credible since "meaning is made by the individual and is dependent on the individual's previous and current knowledge structure" (Merriam and Caffarella, 1999, p. 261).

With regards to assumption #3, adults' readiness to learn can largely be based on an individual's social and occupational role or "what knowledge is of interest" (Merriam and Caraffella, 1999, p. 261); Baumgartner (2003) writes, for instance, that "when Sara enters her company's Japanese headquarters, she is probably more interested in learning job expectations and workplace culture than knowing about the history of the company or retirement plans" (p. 7). Assuming Sara is undergoing a new employee orientation, due to her starting a new position in the human resource development department (HRD), applying this new knowledge as soon as possible is in her best interest; it can also speak to her level and type of motivation (assumption #5). Previous knowledge, experience, personal interests, and a readiness to learn something new about Japanese organizational culture prepare Sara for a new set of propositions (antithesis) that will challenge her preexisting notions, assumptions, and expectations concerning Japanese organizations; experiential learning discourse options can help manage the discovery or meaning making process.

THE DIALECTICAL ANTITHESIS AND EXPERIENTIAL LEARNING

An *antithesis* has been defined as "an equally assertible and apparently contradictory proposition" (Randon House, Webster Dictionary, 1999). As technology, knowledge, and culture are not static, apparent contradictions will always arise to challenge, or enforce, knowledge, ideals, or expectations that were designed to ensure the pursuit of, among other things, "happiness." Indeed, according to Merriam and Caffarella (1999), in response to "life's inherent contradictions and complexities, . . . dialectical ways of thinking must become a part of the ways adults think" (p. 151). One sobering example applies to the American experience; for instance, if according to the *Declaration of Independence* all men are created equal (thesis), then why were others under the yoke of slavery (antithesis)? Obviously, many of our elites in the political and legal system were not thinking ethically—or morally for that matter.

One of the crucial aims of individualist constructivist teaching approaches is to "induce cognitive conflict and hence encourage learners to develop new knowledge schemes that are better adapted to experience. Practical activities supported by group discussions form the core of such pedagogical practices" (Driver et al., 1994, p. 6); the latter activity completes the learning process through social constructivism. As such, antithetical propositions produce the necessary cognitive dissonance for the individual to begin to reconsider, or change, attitudes and consequent behaviors, but it occurs more comprehensively within a communal experiential learning context where debate, disputation, and reflection can occur more effectively. If a dialectical curriculum can serve as a blueprint for constructing a new cognitive learning structure, then experiential learning constructs serve to define actual dialogue specifications that can often lead to the development of positive learning synthesis among adult learners.

In general, experiential learning begins when, for instance, Sara and her student peers undertaking a human resources development course, and guided by an instructor, discuss an article(s) about Japan's changing "social compact" emerging between employees and their employers. According to Dunfee and Yukimasa (1993),[112] the *Ethics of Reciprocity* applied in Japanese organizations required that a balance between benefits and sacrifices be made. Indeed, it had been the case (thesis) since the end of WWII that, due to the close relations between the private and public sectors in Japan, domestic firms were able to offer lifetime employment to their employees; globalization and an aging workforce is changing this employment arrangement and, at a deeper level, impacting the longstanding cultural assumptions about work, thus creating a seeming contradiction (antithesis) for many within and without Japanese society.

Next, using an analysis framework provided by their instructor, Sara's student cohort engages in brainstorming activities centered on how they think longstanding Japanese workers will assimilate the new employment compact given sociological, technological,

---

[112] Dunfee, T. W. and Nagayasu, Y. *Business Ethics: Japan and the global economy*. Norwell: Kluwer Academic Publishers, 1993. Print.

ecological, economic, and political environments. Third, given these five analysis areas, the group is now able to hypothesize about a new set of assumptions Japanese workers may have to begin to accept about their employment and social relationships. Fourth, active experimentation on the part of Sara's student cohort will use the case-study methods about how other Japanese firms, other Asian societies, and the United States began to implement an employment social compact that allowed for often difficult but constructive changes.

Finally, positive synthesis for Sara and Japanese workers can only occur if the resulting new employment compact has taken into consideration the best of previous employment benefits and expectations designed to offer just and equitable employment relationships.

IMPLICATIONS FOR PRACTICE AND FUTURE RESEARCH

Globalization continues to impact the working lives of adults domestically and abroad. This accelerating global phenomenon has made lifelong learning for most adult employees a quasi-compulsory requirement if they expect to remain or offer marketable knowledge, skills, or the preferred attitudes. As such, learning for adult students must continue to remain relevant to their "real world" requirements (e.g., aligned with organizational goals) for the most part, and this demands continual review and revision of curricular designs which enable crucial learning objectives to be achieved.

Relevant curricular *content* appropriate for twenty-first century adult learners must include learning objectives which involve their evolving experiences, relate to workplace tasks, and enable them to apply academic tools and concepts to workplace requirements. The *form* of adult-appropriate curricular designs can include dialectical frameworks which serve as "validating mechanisms" addressing crucial subject matter. It has been my experience that dialectical exchanges can be accomplished within experiential learning (constructivist) contexts wherein students' previously held expectations and assumptions can be positively challenged with new and emerging realities and where the beginning of enlightened synthesis can be achieved about crucial subject matter issues.

But can transformational learning occur within all students? It can if the major curricular elements require all students to apply course tools and concepts to a real-world, workplace problems or challenges. Ideally, course-related major project assignments should include team-based, cross-functional collaboration experiences, indeed, requiring online or Web-based technologies and platforms; this, of course, relates to the real world wherein employee-students are increasingly required to collaborate with their colleagues across time and space at work. As such, what seems to be missing in the literature about twenty-first century adult learners is how a dialectical process can occur via online or within virtual teaching and learning environments. This is an area that must be investigated and researched at greater lengths and depths.

Higher learning also can indeed be considered to be a relative concept based, again, on time, place, and culture. What higher learning represents depends on whether we live in a developed society, meaning organized under a rule of law, or in less developed societies around the world where implicit customary practices, not explicit procedural practices, mainly determine how society's benefits and responsibilities are experienced. While there exists varying types of higher learning, meaning-defined curricula, and degree structures, between developed and less developed societies on the globe, suffice it to say that usually within the latter case less formal, albeit traditional, forms of higher learning occur which address less defined forms of the worldly dimensions stated below; this learning often includes metaphysical, if not inclusion of, supposed supernatural dimensions about the nature of reality.

WORLDLY DIMENSIONS

A multidimensional world seems more explicit and organized for those individuals living in the most developed parts of the world, increasingly so for those in the rapidly developing world but less so for those in the least developed parts of the globe as defined by global organizations like the Organization for Economic Cooperation and Development. Beginning with the most developed nations where oddly enough, but not surprisingly, the meaning of life is hardly understood in light of the multiplicity of stimuli, ubiquitous materialism, and economic demands and challenges occurring in their societies, a rediscovery of the perennial ideas pertaining to the meaning of a truly happy way of life has potential.

In the developing world, where oftentimes there is a greater commitment by political and economic leaders to low-wage job creation within dehumanizing work environments, ancient traditions and thought as found in Confucian teaching, which represents a form of classical learning curricula, still inform East Asian societies, such as China, about the need for correct social cultivation and conduct; interesting to note is that in places like Singapore, the liberal arts curriculum is making inroads into a diverse Asian society that values openness and critical reasoning.

Or readings of the Bhagavad Gita in South Asian countries like India can serve to sustain a nature of reality where right action is informed by obligation ethics and psychological introspection. Both of these major civilizations, in addition to Russia, Brazil, and South Africa, are reemerging and expected to play key roles in the global geo-political spheres and actually challenge the socio-political and economic dominance of the Western world.

In the least developed parts of the world, ancient superstitions and cultural practices pertaining to supposed animist dimensions of nature, gods of nature, the view of women as men's property, and honor killing codes among tribal peoples still inform the daily lives of simple but complex human beings. The lack of adequate transportation and communications infrastructures also creates a precarious daily life for inhabitants in these enduring societies. Moreover, unequal access to fresh water sources for drinking or agriculture purposes has for a millennia been the source of deadly conflict between tribal groups; as such, legitimate state institutions perceived to be just in applying forms of common law within geographical regions is necessary for creating greater social, political, and economic harmony. Higher learning in the least developed parts of the world is mainly delivered by politically or religiously connected leaders who usually tell their students *what* to think instead of *how* to think about ontological issues affecting their lives and communities.

Ultimately, learning should produce a certain level of *change* within humans' cognitive, psycho-motor, or affective dimensions, and this change can be often measured using various evaluation tools as in formative or summative assessments. Stated in another way, for a learning experience to be complete and transferable, learners' mind, body, and spirit must be drawn from and informed further where and when appropriate. Effective learning, therefore, contributes to intentional efforts in self-improvement or what is known in philosophy as *perfectibility*.

Demonstrating how to think about and understand the various dimensions of our world is what generally differentiates between the less educated from the more educated person. Formal, and oftentimes informal, liberal learning experiences can earn an individual the recognition of an educated citizen.

AN EDUCATED CITIZEN

Defining what an educated person is involves many conceptions and controversy in some academic and nonacademic circles. According to the Collins English Dictionary (2003), an educated person generally displays culture, knowledge, and taste;

essentially, the educated individual is cultivated.[113] It seems that an educated person also should have been taught *how* to think, and not simply *what* to think, about life's many issues. Specifically, the educated person can be characterized as the following:

> An educated person should not be a copy of the educated person of a decade ago, or of his or her roommate, or of a student from another part of the country. An educated person should be that highly individualized person, complete in his or her cultural traditions, intellectual emphases, and human interactive possibilities. The truly educated person cannot be described by a score on a standardized national test, but rather by the contribution he or she has made to the lives of other human beings, in both intellectual and social fields.[114]

It seems that at Michigan State University, their philosophy about what an educated person *is* is subject to change over time, not based on standardized testing, and such a person should be other centric. A panel discussion sponsored by Harvard University's Graduate School of Education offered an informal definition of what an educated person can exhibit including competencies in "complex problem-solving, creativity, entrepreneurship, the ability to manage themselves, and the ability to be lifelong learners" (http://www.gse.harvard.edu/news-impact/2012/04/watch-the-askwith-forum-live-defining-the-educated-person/). The latter concept of lifelong learning relates to Rousseau's idea on perfectibility, which extends our understanding of what an educated person can exhibit, be it for the sheer pleasure of learning or for professional purposes.

---

[113] "Educated." Collins English Dictionary. Web. 1/01/2003. (http://www.thefreedictionary.com/educated).

[114] "Educated Person." Michigan State University. Web. 22 Apr. 2014 (http://acadgov.msu.edu/crue/dedication-.html).

According to the Association of American Colleges and Universities report entitled *Becoming an Educated Person: Towards a Core Curriculum for College Students*, all college students should acquire the following skills and attributes (Table 1 below):

Table 1: Becoming an Educated Person

First, they should learn crucial habits of mind: inquiry, logical thinking, and critical analysis. Those aren't taught in any one class; rather, they are built up and refined over time as the student sees how great minds have wrestled with questions in many different fields of knowledge.
Second, they should become literate—proficient in their reading, writing, and speaking. Literacy is a vital and increasingly overlooked component of education that should not be regarded as the exclusive province of the English department.
Third, students should become familiar with quantitative reasoning. In a world filled with numbers and statistics, responsible citizenship calls for an understanding of the correct, and incorrect, uses of numerical data.
Fourth, they should have the perspective on human life that only history can give. People with a grasp of Western civilization, world history, and American history are much better able to see the complexity, uncertainty, and limitations inherent in the human condition. They understand the long struggle to create free and civilized societies. Knowing how we have gotten to our present situation is valuable in comprehending where society may, and can, go in the future.

Fifth, every culture has contributed to the rich repository of human experience. In an interconnected world, it is important to study cultures that maybe very different from our own.

Sixth, students should have an understanding of the natural world and of the methods the sciences use to explore that world. They also need to appreciate what sorts of questions are susceptible of scientific inquiry and which are not.

Seventh, to prepare themselves to become citizens, they should study the American political system and principles articulated in the country's great founding documents

Eighth, to prepare themselves to participate successfully in a dynamic economy, they should study economics and such basic principles as the law of supply and demand.

Ninth, they should learn something about art, music and aesthetics. Besides adding greatly to the enjoyment of life, a study of the arts shows the importance of disciplined creativity.

Tenth, in an increasingly interdependent world, students should learn a foreign language.

Thus, from the preceding descriptions of what, in general, an educated person should have knowledge of, we can say that he or she must be must have a personal competency in critical reasoning, deep literacy, quantitative reasoning, knowledge of history, concepts of cross-cultural competency, the natural sciences, political sciences, economics, appreciation of the arts, and an interest or development of more than one language.

There are definite complementary and competing worldly dimensions in the developed and developing societies where their sociological, technological, economic, and political dimensions can serve to stabilize their transition back into a geo-political world system they did not largely create. Table 2 below serves as a template to initiate and develop further an advanced form of interdisciplinary mindset; in fact, this template attempts to serve as the bridge connecting interdisciplinary theory with practice in the world. Moreover, this template, applied dialogically, is an educational tool which aids the learner and teacher in engaging, interacting, and acquiring knowledge of other cultures, countries, or world civilizations. The use of acronyms can serve this purpose more intentionally and effectively. A basic academic definition is provided along with initiating questions that can launch dialogue and deeper discussions in a formal or informal learning context.

Table 2: STEEPE Analysis: Advanced Interdisciplinary Approach

SOCIOLOGICAL	
Definition	This dimension can encompass the analysis of a particular society, its social institutions, and the diverse social relationships generally associated within a country, or region by extension.

Basic Initiating Questions	What are the group culture dynamics (e.g., attitudes, values, beliefs) inherent within the region or country? How do formal and informal institutions relate to men, women, children, or underrepresented groups?
	What are the historical experiences or current relevant issues, involving men and women, children, religion, race and ethnic groups, languages, and forms of education within the region?
TECHNO-SOCIAL	
Definition	This dimension involves the analysis of what can be basically defined as the tangible products resulting from scientific discovery, breakthrough, or innovation which enable greater social and cultural interaction (i.e., social media) among outer and intra-actors within a region or country.

Basic Initiating Questions	What are the technological issues (communications, transportation systems, community infrastructures) that facilitate social relationships within the region or country? What is the technological level of the region's communications-computer systems and infrastructure? How advanced is the region's railroad, highway, seaport, and air transportation system which connect diverse peoples?
ECOLOGICAL	
Definition	Broadly understood here, this dimension can be defined as those issues relating to the indigenous character of the geography, climate, plant and animal kingdoms, water resources, and level of natural and man-made pollution residing within a certain region or country.

Basic Initiating Questions	What are the issues relating to weather patterns, plant or vegetation, animal populations, terrain, and access to clean water within the region or country? What are the laws and treaties applying to the ecology in this country?
ECONOMIC	
Definition	This dimension can be defined here as those efforts involved in the exploitation of foreign and domestic materials, technologies, and markets used in producing, distributing, and making affordable a society's desired products and services.
Basic Initiating Questions	What are the market and financial forces in play within the region or country? Are there forms of credit, monetary, and fiscal mechanisms manifesting in the economic system?

	Are there forms of underground markets, and what groups are generally controlling them? What are the services or product distribution networks like?
POLITICAL	
Definition	This dimension can be defined as those legitimate, or illegitimate, governing bodies operating within a particular culture, society, or country designed to organize the exercise of power and various governing authorities.
Basic Initiating Questions	How is power exercised or distributed, and through what institutions or networks, within the region or country? Is power exercised generally through totalitarian, authoritarian, or democratic institutions and leadership styles?

ETHICAL	
Definition	This dimension can be understood as those moral philosophies and justice-based practices which *should* be applied to relationships and decisions intended to produce the most honoring or equitable outcomes for members of a society. It is important to state that what in one society may be legal or considered moral may not necessarily be considered ethical in another as community "mores" are typically established by those monopolizing power often to the detriment of others.
Basic Initiating Questions	What are the ethics constructs (e.g., teleological, utilitarian, deontological, or just-war theory) that may apply to analysis of the region or country? How can we achieve the greatest benefit for the majority of the population through our actions within the region or country? In what ways are we duty bound to accomplish a mission that may not be initially clear or popular among powerful interests?

	What indigenous ethical constructs are typically applied within the region or country?

Usually in the West, these aforementioned six dimensional classifications are placed under two major academic categories namely the Arts and Sciences, which are the essential pillars of an undergraduate liberal arts education. Understanding better these and other key dimensions can help citizens to know what specific dynamics impact their lives but, most importantly, how these major worldly dimensions intersect to produce, for better or worse, outcomes in their postmodern world. Knowing how to make better choices in the work of life is what the philosophically informed learning enterprise attempts to achieve at the individual and multidimensional levels of the world. William Cronon, professor of history, writes, "More than anything else, being an educated person means being able to see connections that allow one to make sense of the world and act within it in creative ways" [115]

Therefore, it can be said that a liberal learning represents a canonized or a curricular form of higher learning, which esteems and disseminates knowledge and wisdom about the interdisciplinary worldly dimensions that continue to be relevant to contemporary life in the West and increasingly so for the Far East like China, Singapore, and South Korea. The liberal arts, in concert with the humanities, social sciences, natural sciences, and applied sciences, offer the opportunity to educators at all levels to contribute to a more educated and humane citizen.

---

[115] William Cronon. Only Connect...The Goals of a Liberal Education. *The American Scholar, Vol. 67, No. 4, Autumn 1998.*

BACK TO THE FUTURE

During the late fifth and early fourth century Greece, where foreign sophists, political elites, and priests handed down to the people what they were to accept as true for their lives, a new emphasis about discovering through reason how free citizens should live their lives came to fruition. Through Socrates, the existing focus on philosophical questions pertaining only to the atomistic structures of nature, for instance Thales's ideas that all earthly matter has water as its base, would shift dramatically into a more humanistic arena. The new arena of philosophical focus would be the soul of the human being and how the examined individual could create new questions, experience cognitive dissonance, and through this experience generate better answers to life's questions from within.

During this era, the nascent philosophical field of *epistemology* would gather intellectual steam. Indeed, as Athenian democracy seemed to advance, the need for aspiring political leaders to be adept at employing *rhetoric,* defined simply as the art of persuasion, was increasing. The lack of formal training in rhetoric for free ambitious Athenians became a business opportunity for Sophists from lands as far as Sicily in the west or Melos to the east of Greece.

In particular, it would be as a result of rhetoric in the Athenian social and political contexts, as taught by the itinerant Sophists, who would signal the increasing need for thinking critically about what Athenians took for granted or listened to. Socrates, the Athenian Peloponnesian war veteran, would initiate the free Athenian citizen into the first age of reason not within the confines of a classroom but within the streets and marketplaces of the city. Indeed, within this philosopher's toolbox would be a reasoning tool called critical thinking; this reasoning tool would be essential for engaging in dialogue about life's many issues encountered within the sociological context. This would be true then as it is now.

CHAPTER 5

CRITICAL THINKING: INITIATION

"Read not to contradict and confute; nor to
believe and take for granted; nor to find talk
and discourse; but to weigh and consider."

Francis Bacon, English essayist
"Of Studies," 1625

🦉 🦉 🦉

The roots of the early forms of critical thinking among free citizens were found in ancient Greece (circa fifth century BC). Prominent among this nascent critical reasoning environment in Athens were ongoing dialogues and debates involving Socrates, itinerant wisdom teachers known as Sophists, young elite males, and the free citizens of the city. The Sophists' training methods, in particular, were based on *intellectual Machiavellianism*, that is, using approaches to train and encourage the young, in particular, to achieve worldly success through the unethical use of words, thinking, and rhetoric; this approach certainly appealed to ambitious albeit powerless youngsters but must have deeply concerned some of the guardians like Socrates in the Greek city-state of Athens.

While it is true that Athens is the birthplace of Democracy, most of the residents were slaves. Work was considered to be a curse within Athenian society, and thus, there was a need to replenish the workforce through war booty or through its many noncitizen *émigrés* from abroad. However, while it was the case generally that many free Athenian citizens owned their slaves, the former were nonetheless captives, in an intellectual and spiritual sense, to the ruling elites of Athens; while many Athenian citizens did participate on juries and in elections within the polis, they were not allowed to critically question Athens's religion, with its biased, arbitrary, and capricious gods.

Athens during the late fifth and early fourth centuries had been a time and place of tragedies and hopes for its inhabitants. The Peloponnesian War had recently come to an end (404 BCE), with the consequence of having established illiberal Sparta as the regional superpower. This event also enabled the Thirty Tyrants, a pro-Spartan oligarchy, to suspend the nascent democratic enterprise in Athens for nearly a year before it was restored through the Phyle Campaign. The Athenian cultural ethos leading up to this tragic period was centered on the shallow idea that it was only beauty, strength, and intelligence which characterized virtue in life. Ultimately, Athenian society had committed civilizational overreach, in that in order for its cultural and material prosperity to continue, it had to expand its resources acquisition strategies further afield throughout the Greek isles, and this required brutal military campaigns.

Moreover, leading up to the Athenian defeat by the Spartans, Athens had welcomed many itinerant teachers from Sicily and other places, and none were more popular than the Sophists. As Sophists were known for their ability to teach their students how to use rhetoric in unethical ways, many of Athens' emerging democratic leaders became more adept at winning debates using weak or deceptive rhetoric than in engaging in a search for truth to benefit the *polis*. Young Athenian boys, the pride and future of Athens, were thus being corrupted by the Sophists by developing in them a regressive, rather than a critical and progressive, habit of mind; this type of educational process prevented Athenians from learning how to actually critically analyze the irrational and corrupt assumptions underpinning Athens's fifth century BCE culture. The time had come to begin changing Athenian culture to a way of life based on better thinking and the good; Socrates would begin this shift and initiate many Athenians into the first Age of Reason.

SOCRATES AND NEW WAYS OF THINKING

The entry of Socrates, considered now to be the father of critical inquiry, into the marketplace of ideas marked the beginning of a the West's commitment to reason and dialogue as the more appropriate tool of persuasion for the free citizen, not only capricious political or religious power. This had an empowering effect in that the average citizen without elite political power could influence the course of events in the *polis* or in their local communities. He would prove to be the fallen hero of his time by countering the Sophists' influence and exposing the old order's hypocrisy. If intellectual Machiavellianism was the emerging and popular Sophist teaching and learning approach, then Socrates would respond with a dialogical educational method intended to democratize knowledge construction, or what philosophy calls epistemology, at the street level.

DIALOGUE'S VALUE

Engaging in productive dialogical experiences about important questions, the meaning of life, ethical dilemmas, or shared tasks or problems is not usually a natural human inclination. Certain kinds of dialogue may lead to unsettling outcomes or threaten someone's influence or power. Most knowledgeable individuals realize, sooner or later, that possessing hidden information and pieces of relevant knowledge confers upon them a certain magnitude of power, influence, or control within various social systems like a community or an organization. Creating dialogical environments where crucial tacit knowledge can be made explicit and shared amongst peers is difficult absent some form of coercive force, incentives, or egotistical inclinations on the part of know-it-alls.

Be that as it may, most dialogical exchanges certainly should be experienced within a social context in order for old and emerging ideas to receive the necessary and fair scrutiny; subsequent application in the abstract or real world is often the consequence of such a dialogical process. Emmanuel Kant was adamant about this point in that, while reason should continue to have a role in the development of new ideas, personal intuitions should, nonetheless, be recognized and explored within community in order for them to gain validity and influence at some level.

Socrates was able to create a sense of buy-in, and a subsequent feeling of ownership to an idea, among a group of interested and engaged participants; he accomplished this through a dialogical, versus monological, form of examination based on early forms of critical inquiry. But it seems that as this form of dialogue progressed, a type of cognitive dissonance would inevitably take place and was actually instrumental in creating new light exposing the blind spots in a person's thinking or operating assumptions. In the contemporary sense what we postmodernists understand as a dialectical process, a more formal dialogical experience can provide for a validating mechanism that is necessary for intentional cognitive dissonance to take place during critical analysis of important issues.

Due to his epistemological approaches, Socrates's dialogical approach would expose the actual blind ignorance of the proverbial know-it-alls of the Athenian city-state; this would make him many enemies as much as create many more admirers, especially amongst young men. In fact, as the wisest man in Athens, Socrates knew of the importance of demonstrating intellectual humility, genuinely or by pretending, to convey the idea that he did not know all the answers to life's crucial questions as a cult leader might; this would lead to an unhealthy dependence on him by his audiences or followers. On the other hand, his increasing number of enemies believed they were omniscient but ignorant of the fact that they were not. For a price, the Sophists would add to the human problem of egocentric thinking by teaching their students how to sound omniscient and with convincing tones. Socrates would be resented for drawing out revelations of blind ignorance at no charge, but for high tuition fees, the Sophists' would develop one's ability to leverage and exploit egocentric thinking and discourse. By reflecting on history, we can discern that egocentric thinking and belief systems that inform critical social decisions tend to create more dysfunction than progress in society, indeed, total breakdown through war in the worst-case scenarios.

In the end, Socrates would pay with his life, having been charged by the authorities of corrupting the youth of Athens by teaching them how to think for themselves or examine others' ideas. Historian Bettany Hughes writes that the young men of Athens, in particular, were considered to be the city-state's greatest national security resource as it would be the young men of Athens that would defend and conduct foreign military campaigns on behalf of the nascent democracy; corrupting their views about the gods of Athens, Athenian patriotism, or teaching them how to examine the hegemonic assumptions of Athenian society was a threat to the long-term vital interests of Athenian hegemonic ambitions of empire.[116]

However, the far greater threat to the key Athenian elites was Socrates's questioning of the idea that a true god engaged in acts of evil at all. According to Plato's *Republic*, Socrates is depicted as recommending that the ideal state censor the poets and works like Homer's *Iliad* which depicts the gods as capricious, biased, unethical, and ultimately as harmful examples to the youth and adults of Athens. Banning such works of influential poetry would thus, over time, have the effect of discrediting the elite's justification for committing their own acts of evil on earth as godly deeds demanded only good deeds be committed within human domains. Indeed, Socrates is quoted as saying that "since the god is good . . . He and he alone must be held responsible for good things,

---

[116] Hughes, Bettany. *The Hemlock Cup: Socrates, Athens and the Search for the Good Life.* New York: Vantage Books, 2012. Print.

but responsibility for bad things must be looked for elsewhere and not attributed to the god."[117]

And so we see that for a religious leader, or monarch invoking the divine right of kings, to assert the example of the gods as sufficient reason to engage in war on their less than righteous neighbors because "god" told them seems grossly irrational, if not criminal. What is not addressed in this dialogue, however, is the danger of banning or censoring information and knowledge in a free society; but Plato was not necessarily recommending in his dialogues that his students establish an open democratic society. What is crucial for members of a free society is that they have the opportunity to critically analyze and evaluate the pertinent evidence involved in peculiar cases, new ideas, or public policy. So what does a philosophical argument addressing the issue of requiring necessary evidence for important decisions look like? Two gentlemen would philosophically debate this central human and social issue during the late nineteenth century.

The debate in question involved W.K. Clifford and William James. The issue of valid evidence is outlined as follows: Clifford claimed that "it is wrong always, everywhere, and for anyone, to believe anything upon insufficient evidence." James objected that this view "is not intellect against all passions, then; it is only intellect with one passion laying down its law."

Clifford, an English philosopher and mathematician, posited his claims about justified belief during the late 1870s, around the same period that the faculty of theology and natural philosophy parted ways in much of the English-speaking world but, in particular, on many college campuses across the United States; the gospel of empiricism was finally replacing unexamined means for justifying many sacred and all secular beliefs. James, an American philosopher and psychologist, would respond to Clifford's seeming dogmatism concerning the need for sufficient evidence to justify all

---

[117] Hughes, Bettany. *The Hemlock Cup: Socrates, Athens and the Search for the Good Life*. New York: Vantage Books, 2012, p. 134. Print.

beliefs by claiming that sometimes it is fine to believe *some* things without strong corroborating evidence.

THE DISPUTE

According to Clifford, "it is wrong always, everywhere, and for anyone, to believe anything upon insufficient evidence." It seems that Clifford makes no room for the supernatural, superstition, miracles, or emotional manipulation as a way to justify beliefs in one's or others' lives. In fact, he argues that if an individual does not operate under a belief that was a result of investigation, the sense of power or pleasure he derives from a new belief is a stolen one and in defiance of a certain solemn duty to mankind. Clifford writes that ultimately, this duty "is to guard ourselves from such beliefs as from a pestilence, which may shortly master our own body and then spread to the rest of the town."[118]

Clifford's other concern was that, as a result of operating under unjustified beliefs, a society of gullible or credulous citizens would eventually emerge. Clifford states, "The danger to society is not merely that it should believe wrong things, though that is great enough; but that it should become credulous, and lose the habit of testing things and inquiring into them; for then it must sink back into savagery";[119]Plato's allegory of the cave comes to mind when Clifford refers to sinking back into savagery or intellectual darkness. Moreover, Clifford makes reference to testing ideas, like a hypothesis, as through the scientific method that can produce light and progress, in addition to, the need to Socratically inquire into matters of consequence, and this included the sacred cow of religious belief.

---

[118] Clifford, W.K. The Ethics of Belief. In *Reason and Responsibility, Readings in Some Basic Problems in Philosophy, 14ᵗʰ Edition*. Eds. Joel Feinberg and Russ Shafer-Landau. New York: Wadsworth Publishing, 2013, p. 120. Print.

[119] Ibid, p. 121.

However, James disagrees with Clifford's seeming dogmatic position on what qualifies as justified true belief by making room for emotional influences on some of our decision making. James writes, "Our passional nature not only lawfully may, but must, decide an option between propositions; whenever it is a genuine option between propositions, whenever it is a genuine option that cannot by its nature be decided on intellectual grounds; for to say, under such circumstances, 'Do not decide, but leave the question open,' is itself a passional decision-just like deciding yes or no—and is attended with the same risk of losing truth."[120] James suggests here that sometimes it is appropriate for our emotional or affective dimension to inform a decision pertaining to important options even if we don't have full corroborating evidence; but they must be genuine options, not the manipulation that Pascal's Wager offers, described by James as the "last desperate snatch at a weapon against the hardness of an unbelieving heart."[121] If we don't make room for passional influences on our decision making, then we stand to lose a truth that benefits both believer and nonbeliever alike.

James further argues that our intellect does not always regulate what we believe; oftentimes we are impressed by the prestige of certain subjects or subject matter expertise, and we suspend the critical thinking skills we must apply to what we listen to or read about; in this regard, Clifford may agree with James. This is often the case with religious leaders (e.g., Rev. Jim Jones, Pope's Crusades, or David Koresh). However, there are some religious beliefs that may have some good to benefit from. These might include the Golden Rule as spoken by Christ and secularized by Emmanual Kant's Category Imperative, with the former influencing the latter so as to make religious truth emotionally appealing and beneficial to nonbelievers.

Both Clifford and James seem to agree, however, that it is crucial to enable reason to reign over faith or emotions in all, if

---

[120] James, William. The Will to Believe. In *Reason and Responsibility, Readings in Some Basic Problems in Philosophy, 14th edition*. New York: Wadsworth Publishing, 2013, p. 125. Print.

[121] Ibid, p. 124.

not in most, cases. Clifford emphatically states that should a man hold a belief from childhood or acquire one in adulthood but yet refuse to confront his doubts about it, due to confirmation bias or by refusing to consider new data, this man misses the mark entirely with mankind. Indeed, James writes, "Let us agree, however, that whenever there is no forced option, the *dispassionately judicial intellect* with no pet hypothesis, saving us, as it does, from dupery at any rate, ought to be our ideal" (emphasis mine).

While Clifford's insistence on sufficient evidence is important for decisions involving religious practice, scientific and public policy issues that will impact animals, humans, and natural resources, he does not seem to recognize that there are important cases where some religious beliefs may be beneficial for society, including for those that consider themselves to be agnostic or nonbelievers. Most of the Ten Commandments, Christ's Golden Rule—of which many variations are found in many cultures—or Hinduism and Buddhism's concern for all living creatures and Islam's encouragement to charitable giving can be used as examples of where there is no need for sufficient intellectual evidence for mankind to accept as a beneficial true belief, based especially on universal values. Nonetheless, religious beliefs can never be used to condemn others for their refusal to accept something they cannot see, touch, or hear.

James, on the other hand, fails to realize that Clifford may not be coming from a "passional" place of *fear* of error but perhaps instead from a passional place for the *love* of wisdom or truth. In a court of law, it is only sufficient evidence that can potentially count toward proof (truth) of the innocence or guilt of an individual, which leads to a decision by a judge or jury; justice is seemingly served. Oftentimes, crafty sophistic lawyers attempt to sway the emotions, or passions, of the jury in order to persuade them about an untruth, regardless of sufficient evidence against a defendant. As James himself suggests, our "dispassionate judicial intellect . . . ought to be our ideal" when attempting to justify what we consider to be true belief.

CRITICAL THINKING IN PRACTICE

If Socrates was right in the idea that the unexamined life is not worth living, then it can be safe to assume also that the unexamined belief, proposition, situation, or circumstance is not worth engaging in within the personal and sociological context; this thus requires questioning the assumptions that underpin authoritative and common ideas. Central to questioning authority and existing assumptions of what we currently think we know is an application of critical thinking skills; indeed, central to contemporary goals of liberal learning objectives is the cultivation of critical thinking skills.

In a Faculty Lecture delivered by Rebecca Chopp, president of Swarthmore College, entitled *Against the Grain: Liberal Arts in the 21st Century,* important research findings of the continuing relevance of critical thinking were discussed. She states:

> First, critical thinking, rather than mastery of technical or codified knowledge, is the heart and soul of a liberal arts education. Critical thinking requires that teachers encourage students to refine their capacity for analytic thinking; ask difficult questions and formulate responses; evaluate, interpret, and synthesize evidence; make clear, well-reasoned arguments; and develop intellectual agility. Critical thinking is not only good for the individual but also beneficial for society-the common good flourishes through an ongoing expansion of intellectual capital that is both self-critical and innovative. [122]

---

[122] Chopp, Rebecca. *Against the Grain: Liberal Arts in the 21st Century.* Web. 1 April 2014. (http://www.swarthmore.edu/presidents-office/against-the-grain---liberal-arts-in-the-21st-century.xml.)

For Professor Chopp, critical reasoning abilities are at the heart of liberal learning and crucial for communicating important ideas in society. Critical thinking can be defined simply as the process of analyzing and evaluating credible data, information, and the assumptions that underpin what we currently *know* about the accepted reality in our worlds. As philosophy enables us to engage in a search for truth using cognitive standards, its partner conception, the *love* of *wisdom*, demands that we as well include the affective dimensions, namely that effective critical reasoning involves the application of both the emotional (affective) and reasoning (cognitive) traits. When both traits are effectively employed during dialogical exchanges, more ethical forms of communications tend to take place. Thus, at the core of the critical thinking competency are what Paul and Elder (2009) call the intellectual standards (IS) and the intellectual traits (IT), the former considered the cognitive and the latter the affective dimensions to critical thinking competency.

To begin with, the intellectual standards represent a designated taxonomy designed to focus critical thinking during the analysis of what we are thinking about, writing about, listening to, or reading. The intellectual standards' vocabulary includes the universal concepts of clarity, precision, accuracy, relevancy, depth, breadth, logicality, significance, and fairness (see Table 1 below).

THE INTELLECTUAL STANDARDS

Paul and Elder posit what they consider are universally accepted ways of thinking critically concerning what we hear, read, and write about; it is assumed that with these "universal" intellectual standards all individuals communicating in good faith find it in their enlightened self-interest to apply, indeed expect from others the same standards. Philip Regal asserts, however, that the idea of common sense, often considered a universal experience, may not necessarily be so as this form of understanding is dependent on culture, time, and context.[123] In any event, by universal intellectual standards, Paul and Elder (2008) mean acknowledging and applying to analysis a taxonomy that includes the standards of clarity, precision, accuracy, relevance, depth, breadth, logic, significance, and fairness.[124] Essentially, filtering what we hear, read, and write about through these intellectual standards increases the likelihood that we may arrive at an impermanent "ground truth" as circumstances change more often in our mostly uncertain operating environments requiring more of a reframing mindset that is comfortable with and responds to ambiguity.

Table 3 below reflects the IS terms and corresponding initiating questions, which can be applied, in particular, during teaching sessions, guided discussion, facilitation, and group dialogue experiences in a classroom or occupational setting.

Table 3: Intellectual Standards

Standard	Initiating Questions
Clarity	Could you elaborate, provide an example, or illustrate what you mean (analogy)?
Precision	Could you be more specific, provide more detail, or be more exact using the context?
Accuracy	How could we check, or verify, that this data, information, or intelligence is true?
Relevance	How does this particular data or information relate to the problem, question, or help the issue?
Depth	What factors make the issue difficult or complex? A complex issue requires deeper answers.
Breadth	Do we need to view the issue from another perspective or point of view?

---

123 Philip Regal, "Anatomy of Judgment," (Minnesota, MN: University of Minnesota Press), 89-92.

124 Richard Paul and Linda Elder, "Intellectual Standards: The Words That Name Them and the Criteria That Define Them," (Dillon Beach, CA: Foundation for Critical Thinking Press, 2008), 7-11.

Logic	Does all this data or information make sense together or follow from the evidence?
Significance	What information and knowledge is most important at this time?
Fairness	Are there any vested interests at stake, and are detractors' views represented or being considered?

For instance, a university teacher applying the intellectual standards would ideally induce and develop critical thinking skills by requesting of her students more *clarity* (i.e., definition of terms, examples, or analogies) when explaining a story's basic plot or the main character's thinking in, for instance, Upton Sinclair's book entitled *The Jungle*. One of Socrates's greatest questions to his audiences was to ask for greater clarity about the essential meaning of justice, and by extension social justice. Was justice based on objective criteria applicable to every situation, or was it determined solely, as Thrasymychus would argue, by those who held power in society?

There would also be the criteria of *precision* where a need for precise dates, exact locations, statistics, percentages, and raw numbers is necessary to provide a more detailed or complete picture about an event or situation. On what actual date was the *Declaration of Independence* pronounced? Does the nurse's report indicate the precise body temperature of the sick child in the emergency room? But how can the listener determine the accuracy of the seemingly precise statistics, percentages, or information as forms of sophistry can always be employed to make partisan and propagandist arguments? It has often been stated in jest that *liars figure and figures lie.*

The standard of *accuracy,* therefore, demands that seemingly precise, or compelling, claims be corroborated using other relevant and reliable sources, such as expert testimony or independent testing. Now, a writer can achieve clarity, precision, and accuracy generally, but are all of their claims *relevant* to the central issue or not? For instance, when the central issue being studied or

145

discussed is about social institutions, such as forms of secular government, then relevant concepts such as democracy, monarchy, dictatorship, or oligarchy are strongly related to the discussion but not necessarily religious or private economic institutions.

Applying critical thinking attitude, or a healthy skepticism, to what we write, listen to, or read about also necessitates that a certain level of *depth* of understanding of a content area be evident in our writing, a speaker's words, or a narrative. Is the speaker defining difficult terms or concepts when necessary? Is the writer providing easy answers to complex issues? When the published article about drinking water makes claims about the level of cleanliness, is the study's author characterizing results data as parts-per-million or not? Is she addressing all the relevant variables which make the issue complex? Or is he covering the background, intermediate, and advanced dimensions of an issue at stake?

Breadth is the other intellectual standard that must be met when exploring ideas, dilemmas, or social problems and the appropriate responses to them. This standard requires an interdisciplinary approach. Are the relevant sociological, technological, ecological, economic, political, and ethical dimensions explored by a policy maker when attempting to better understand drug addiction before recommending more comprehensive insights that may inform new laws? Is it evident that the writer or speaker has cited broad but relevant voices affecting an issue? In this intellectual standard, displaying an understanding of multiple perspectives is crucial in demonstrating that as many relevant viewpoints as possible have been considered when studying a complex issue.

The other intellectual standard, *logicality*, requires that any conclusions provided by the speaker, writer, or as a consequence of our own thinking be logical or follow the data or pertinent evidence available in the analysis. Are the writer's concluding remarks and recommendations based on the preceding analysis discussed in the body of the article or lecture? Does the author of a peer-reviewed article recommend further research in an area that was not covered in her analysis? Next, the standard of *significance* must also be met when conveying or documenting data or information to an audience. Thus, it becomes necessary for analysts or experienced practitioners to point out the most important data or information for others to especially consider and demonstrate why; in this case, the standard of relevance and depth of experience informs the selection of what information will be given the most attention especially when time is lacking and a quicker decision must be made during a crisis.

Finally, the intellectual standard of *fairness* to one's critics or detractors is important for many reasons, not the least of which is to demonstrate, in a transparent way, that one understands what the "other side" thinks of one's issue; so, we have demonstrated a level of empathy about what is important to our detractors or the critics of the issue. In addition, we know at some level that our own position on the issue has been strengthened as a consequence of it being subjected to the scrutiny of good-faith detractors. In the final analysis, we have used the weight of our critics to point out the areas of weaknesses in our own thinking or side of the argument.

The intellectual traits, on the other hand, involve human attitudes, and at times the spiritual dimensions, of critical thinking; quite often, these are the more difficult intellectual competencies to develop as they largely relate to our egos, indeed, the threats to our egos. It can be assumed that the intellectual traits are probably the more important critical reasoning competency when engaging in dialogical learning experiences.

THE INTELLECTUAL TRAITS

Paul and Elder (2007) advance the idea that applying critical thinking to important dialogue requires certain intellectual traits (reasoning attitudes) also to be exercised among participants. Indeed, these intellectual traits, the more difficult competencies to develop, seem to elevate the thinking, good will, and information sharing propensities of most participants. Insisting that the intellectual traits be actively involved seems to suggest that thinking critically involves a genuine commitment to respectful or ethical dialogue between parties. These IT include intellectual fair-mindedness, intellectual humility, intellectual courage, intellectual empathy, intellectual perseverance, confidence in reason, intellectual autonomy, insights into egocentricity, and intellectual integrity. Table 4 below reflects the IT terms and corresponding metacognitive (thinking about our thinking) questions, which can be cognitively applied to what we hear, read, and write about.

Table 4: Intellectual Traits

Intellectual	Meta-cognitive Questions
fair-mindedness	Am I giving all rational viewpoints equity and without reference to my own views, biases, and vested interests?
humility	Am I aware of my lack of omniscience and that there will be a new aspect of an issue I will learn about?
courage	Am I willing to listen to a position for which I strongly disagree with? Am I prepared to voice an unpopular viewpoint which may have a social cost?
empathy	Am I able to accept, understand, and regurgitate others' viewpoints without bias?
perseverance	Am I prepared not to give up when analyzing an intellectually complex issue?
confidence in reason	Am I willing to use reason and evidentiary tools to arrive at conclusions while minimizing emotional interference?

autonomy	Am I able to analyze information independent of others' overriding negative influences but use intellectual standards to arrive at my own conclusions?
insights into egocentricity	Am I unaware of my subconscious or unconscious need to be right always, especially when wanting to have my way on an issue?
integrity	Am I expecting others to meet a higher standard of intellectual evidence or proof than I would apply to myself?

With the trait of *fair-mindedness,* there is an attempt on the part of all parties to search for the truth of an issue and not simply attempt to win an argument for their side. Participants to a dialogue must acknowledge the influences of their cloaked interests when arguing key points in a dialogue. Giving all relevant rational viewpoints or contributions to a vital issue quite often requires that we know and sense what statements coming from others are too emotionally laced or a reasonably informed person. Whether its criticism, or proponents contribution in favor of your argument, the idea must be based on rational thinking which ideally contain greater levels of depth and breadth of objective understanding of a certain issue being debated; oftentimes, this is where the sin of intellectual omission is committed.

The trait of intellectual *humility* is that we suspend judgment about an issue being discussed as there is always something new to discover and learn about; indeed, one must be aware of our lack of omniscience during dialogue. What new data or information pertaining to the issue at hand do I stand to learn more about? The trait of intellectual *courage* represents the idea that many times it is important to "hear out" an idea or position that you may really disagree with. Why did this mother of four children decide to have an abortion when she discovered that her pregnancy actually threatened her life during the birthing process? The other crucial aspect to this standard is about expressing a socially unpopular position. So am I prepared to voice a dissenting opinion knowing full well that my position may cost me socially, financially, or career-wise?

The trait of intellectual *empathy* recommends that we be open to understanding the position of a detractor or even an enemy. Am I willing to adequately understand what the concerns of my detractors are? Indeed, am I able to regurgitate my detractor's position without attaching my own biases? The trait of intellectual *perseverance* suggests that many times it is important not to stop the "search" that Socrates talked about; not giving up on important searches or efforts to understand very complex issues is an important human trait. The trait of *confidence in reason* represents the idea that one must have a commitment to using the tools of reason when attempting to analyze and evaluate new and existing information; not allowing the undue interference of emotions like anger, hate, or prejudice is important as its light must emerge, not heat.

The trait of intellectual *autonomy* requires that we rule out or attempt to prevent outside influences on our reasoning. Effective reasoning autonomy is best employed when we use objective, meaning open, intellectual standards to arrive at conclusions. The trait of having *insights to egocentricity* requires that we realize that much of the time when dialoging with others we often insist that our position is the right one and having our own way is what should be the outcome; not a genuine search for the truth which may discredit or expose the weakness in our position. Finally, the trait of intellectual *integrity* recommends that we apply consistent intellectual expectations to others as we would expect of ourselves. The intellectual standards and intellectual traits represent a balance of cognitive and affective reasoning tools that produce better dialogue and understanding between communicating individuals. However, there are also particular impediments to critical thinking that must be explored and dealt with effectively.

IMPEDIMENTS TO CRITICAL THINKING

However important it may be to know, understand, and apply the IT and the IS, leveraging them effectively requires the acknowledgement and subsequent elimination over time of as many thinking impediments as possible; the process of dislodging thinking impediments can be facilitated within an organizational culture that values and sustains a climate of healthy skepticism, high trust, and affords opportunities for more egalitarian-based discussion formats. Robert Carroll recommends considering the following impediments to critical thinking, which are reflected below (see Table 5).[125]

Table 5: Impediments to Critical Thinking

Attitude: not open-minded, skeptical, or tentative about new data or information	**Sense perception:** failing to realize that human senses are limited to some extent
Apophenia: seeing patterns where none exist within an environment under analysis	**Hypersensory perception:** a reliance on only intuitive abilities or behavioral cues
Inattentional blindness: too single-focused on a task, thereby fails to note related key variables	**Worldviews:** moral and religious beliefs filter how we perceive a situation and consider relevant facts
Memory: failing to realize that human memory recall is unreliable	**Testimony:** vivid and compelling accounts made by experts can also be manipulation
Ignorance: lacking sufficient background knowledge on an issue	**Beliefs:** the belief that intelligence and the ability to engage in deep analysis is genetically determined

---

[125] Robert T. Carroll, *Becoming a Critical Thinker: A Guide for the New Millennium* 2nd ed., (Boston, MA: Pearson, 2005), 4-23.

Laziness and pride: resorts to generalizations or stereotypes to understand; too proud to acknowledge lack of understanding	**Suggestibility:** unaware that repeated confident statements made by authority figures can engender flawed faith in the listener's ideas
Admiration for experts: emotional value ascribed to subject matter experts prevents criticism of that expertise	**Bias or prejudice:** unaware that one may respond to information with a cultural, political, religious bias; prejudice occurs when preconceived notions inform understanding, not evidence
Confirmation bias: seeks only data/information that confirms personal bias but ignores contradicting data or information	**Emotional hindrances:** unaware that anger, fear, or jealousy can distort information processing or understanding
Censorship: superiors and others controlling access to key information, preventing full understanding	**Threat of litigation:** the threat of costly litigation or consequences can stifle free speech and its positive or negative consequences
Wishful thinking: interpreting facts and events as one would like them to be, not based on evidence	

As it relates the category of *attitude,* it is also important to consider Aristotle's idea of the mean, or what I call a balanced thinking approach. What this means is that we apply a healthy skepticism to what we read or listen to, arriving at a balance between extreme skepticism (too closed-minded) at one end and extreme gullibility (too open-minded) at the other end.

With regards to *apophenia,* it is important to verify with others that the figure we think we see in the sky or our office wall may not be what we think it is, and much less, used as a sign to inform an important decision. Humans tend to be pattern-seeking creatures, and not realizing this may be detrimental to genuine understanding in the environment; thus, we may ask a trusted friend or colleague, "Do you see the face of George Washington in the tree bark like I do?" *Inattentional blindness* tends to occur when an individual does not apply systems thinking in his or her operating environment. Oftentimes, while focusing too much attention on a major component of a social or operating system, other minor but key components are neglected, hindering understanding of how each key component actually relate to each other systematically. Adopting a habit of asking ourselves questions such as *how will my decisions affect the next department or customer in the supply chain* becomes important. Thus, an ability to engage in multicomponent thinking is required for operating environments' understanding and problem solving.

In the category of *memory,* not realizing that humans do not have perfect recall about what we have experienced or have learned can inadequately inform efforts to understand a new situation or, at worst, cause a travesty of justice as when a witness to a recent crime will claim they can perfectly remember how many perpetrators were involved and which one shot the victim. Asking ourselves before we make critical claims questions like *how can I corroborate what I think I saw and heard with others that were also there* is important as well.

In the category of *ignorance,* an individual, for fear of being exposed as lacking key background knowledge, refuses to ask clarifying questions and, as a consequence, falls into deeper levels of knowledge deficit pertaining to his expertise or an issue that may require her input. Adopting the idea that it is actually a sign of wisdom to ask for background knowledge is called for here. The impediment of *laziness and pride* enables, if not encourages, an individual to resort to generalizations or stereotypes. The refusal to undertake the difficult work, or a proud attitude that prevents a person from admitting to ignorance of others, actually increases the likelihood that personal or cross-cultural *faux pas* will occur when operating in new or foreign contexts. So statements like "You know how they are" become the default thinking modality for many under the influence of this impediment. *Admiration for experts* occurs when an individual's emotional preference for a certain subject matter expert prevents the layperson from applying his or her critical reasoning faculties to what experts may say or write about a certain issue or topic. We may say that a world-renowned expert has to be right in what they're saying because he or she shares the same political ideology as I do or shares the same taste in clothing.

The impediment of *confirmation bias* occurs when an individual will only recognize or affirm data and information that confirms his or her personal preferences while at the same time consciously ignoring any contradictory information. The impediment of *censorship* occurs when leaders or other key actors withhold important or politically sensitive data or information that may actually enlighten a problem or aid in solving a dilemma in a dialogue or organizational problems. The impediment of *wishful thinking* occurs when an individual interprets the outcomes of certain messages or events as they would like them to be understood. We may say in this kind of situation, "The letter from the attorney's office says exactly what I thought."

The impediment of *sense perception* occurs when an individual does not realize that our five sense are often faulty and actually can degrade over our lifetime; thus, a manager in the organization will make decisions based on what he thought he heard in the staff meeting last week. Or someone in a jury pool will state to attorneys, "I have never had the need to use glasses, so my vision can be relied upon as a witness to this accident." The weakness with *hypersensory perception* is that one may rely too much on supposed intuitive abilities. Oftentimes, this is confused with the importance of informing a crucial decision with experience; in this case, however, there is an overreliance on "gut feelings" and undue body language, for instance, that may supposedly confirm an intuition. More concrete evidence is therefore required for all cases.

Having an impediment based on *world views* suggests that a diplomat's moral and religious views may filter how he or she views a negotiation opportunity in a certain part of the world. For instance, if a politician or diplomat believes that, according to the

Bible, a certain ethnic group of a particular region of the world will be destroyed by God, then her level of good-faith commitment will be unreliable as it may disadvantage one of the parties involved in peace negotiations. A certain style of **testimony** delivery may compromise its validity in the minds of many; oftentimes, a subject matter expert of celebrity may deliver an impassioned address before the U.S. Congress but not necessarily provide relevant and important evidence to back up his compelling claims about animal poaching in Africa or child trafficking in Asia. A person's **beliefs** about their intellectual abilities can also be an impediment to critical thinking; some may say, "But I was always told by my father that I was stupid" or "I was always told that math was not for girls because we weren't any good at it."

Operating under the impediment of **suggestibility** is the idea that an individual carrying intense emotional attachments to a person's ideas or words will make the former more susceptible to accepting flawed arguments or information; this can include repeated claims about certain ideas or marketplace products and services. With the impediments of **bias or prejudice** we find an individual who may be unaware that he or she is filtering data and information in what they read, listen to, or interact with using unfounded biases. For instance, such an individual may state that because the new unemployed rate has remained the same, then it confirms his bias that those that are unemployed are simply lazy people wanting to stay on the public dole; perhaps the case is, instead, that many new workers have been laid-off, but also, many previously unemployed persons have found new work within an emerging technology-based industry. This can lead to forms of prejudice for certain groups like some persons of color, the poor, the middle-aged or the non-college educated, meaning we judge these persons situations on unfounded ideas, not facts or evidence.

As it relates to the impediment of **emotional hindrances**, we often misunderstand situations and make bad decisions because we are mad, jealous, fearful, or insecure of others or a situation. And finally, operating under a **threat of litigation** can create information censorship, dampen free dialogue, or prevent any form of positive association among a group of responsible professionals.

While critical thinking can be used responsibly as a powerful tool for analyzing and evaluating many forms of data, information, knowledge, and even what many consider to be wisdom, this reasoning tool can place an individual into a state of unhealthy perpetual skepticism. This often happens because an individual chooses to use critical reasoning as a tool of cynicism instead of a tool for healthy skepticism. What we understand a cynic to be in the contemporary sense is a person that is often not interested in applying the tools of critical reasoning to search for truth *with* his or her detractors but to, usually, win a partisan argument and therefore punish, not correct or assist, others. Positively and productively using the tools of critical reasoning is necessary for engaging in thinking creatively. For most situations requiring new answers or improvement, analysis and evaluation of how things currently exist or operate is important; thus, the process of thinking creatively moves forward without, for instance, reinventing the wheel.

CHAPTER 6

THINKING CREATIVELY: IMAGINATION

Imagination is more important than knowledge.

Albert Einstein

Henry Ford once said that "thinking is the hardest work there is which is the probable reason why so few engage in it."[126] If we're to believe such a controversial figure's words on the general thinking propensities of human beings, then we also might consider the era of American industry during which he made these comments. We can assume that he made these observations during the throes of the early twentieth century industrial era when most workers were paid *to do* and not *to think*.

Certainly, the public education system of the early twentieth century within many of the large metropolitan areas, which contained many non-English speaking immigrant groups, did not provide a basic education in how to think critically, much less on how to think creatively; indeed, many public education systems in major U.S. cities seemed to mirror the factory system, with its many grades (departments), cafeterias, and bells signaling changes

---

[126] Henry Ford. My Life and Work. CreateSpace Independent Publishing Platform. Web. 1 Jan 2014.

throughout the day. During this era, it was your back, not your mind, which represented workplace value to potential employers, many of whom had no regard for workers' health and safety.

Upton Sinclair's book entitled *The Jungle,* published in 1906, depicts seemingly sensational, but often factual, muckraker accounts of the many hazardous workplace conditions that workers operated within at the meat-packing companies in Chicago and about the careless attitudes that management had about the worth of the average under-educated manual laborer during this era. Thus, with a few exceptions, compliance and not thinking were incentivized in the American workplace during this early part of the twentieth century.

Indeed, it would be scientific management guru Frederick Taylor who would help Ford and other industrialists create more efficient production processes at the Ford auto assembly plants and other domestic and international companies. Taylor's scientific management principles ultimately provided for "detailed instruction and supervision of each worker in the performance of that worker's discrete task."[127] As it relates to *perfectibility* in the workforce, meaning the experience of learning new skills and personal development at work, echoes of Karl Marx's words about the real value the worker's contribution represented to the production process must've informed management's operations designs to teach the worker only one "discrete task." Training and developing workers to perform many tasks would conceivably increase a worker's value and bargaining power for better wages and benefits. In the minds of many owners and managers, training workers in one task made them easily replaceable in the labor market, especially if workers struck for better wages or workplace conditions.

It was generally assumed during the first half of the twentieth century that the average blue-collar worker in American society

---

[127] Montgomery, David (1989), *The Fall of the House of Labor: The Workplace, the State, and American Labor Activism, 1865-1925,* Cambridge University Press, Paperback edition, p. 217.

was solely motivated by financial reward and not expected to exhibit the necessary autonomy and intellectual prowess to direct or manage himself in the assembly line. With the exception of the World War II timeframe, most women were not to be found within industrial production plants in the United States. Thus, most of a worker's thinking on the assembly line was accomplished for him by production and operations designs developed by industrial engineers like Taylor and the results of the Frank and Lillian Gilbreth's time and motion studies.

THE CREATIVITY ERA

If it has been the case for most of the industrial age that workers, trained or educated, had most of their thinking done for them by "scientific management," then thinking creatively was much less required, if not discouraged, in the organizational environment. Some of this would change during the 1950s, during which many private sector companies, by employing the marketing concept, began to ask customers what they wanted in terms of benefits and features in their cars, washing machines, or kitchen items. With increased domestic competition, the philosophy of *build it and they'll come* no longer was viable in American capitalism after 1950; the customer was now a creative partner with the private sector employee.

Increasingly, employees in the sales and marketing force or design and engineering department required more critical and creative thinking competencies; the operations and assembly departments or the accounting and finance division required thinking skills to trouble shoot and analyze, and more employees were expected to apply greater amounts of autonomous judgment in the course of their more complex duties. With increased assembly automation, computerization, and international competition in the late twentieth century American workplace, the need for creativity to out innovating domestic and international competitors became a priority for private sector company shareholders and managers.

As many manual operations have been outdated to history or outsourced to lower-wage countries around the globe, many kinds of traditional jobs will never come back to our shores. This has been the case for any nation operating within the global economy; for instance, China has lost jobs to lower wage countries like Viet Nam.

Thinking critically in the workplace has maintained its value, but it has become increasingly obvious that thinking creatively is just as important; the former thinking competency analyzes and evaluates the past and current situations while latter thinking competencies focuses more on how to improve future situations.

Currently within countries containing mainly services and high technology economies, the shift has occurred in management's expectation that new employees and management trainees be better trained or educated about how they think work should be accomplished, especially within the virtual space. Moreover, as certificate or training credentials become outdated sooner rather than later, many employers or employees are finding it too expensive to stay abreast in the skills required to remain competitive in many high-tech industries.

Indeed, in the information age global business arena, economic competition and cross-cultural exchange has made it necessary for better educated workers and managers to partner in efforts to think outside of the traditional boundaries to innovate on existing products and services; thus, thinking creatively requires a partnership involving the final customer, line employees, and management. In fact, purposeful creative thinking requires that organizational leaders begin to view the committed individual employee as endowed with a genius to improve an existing service, product, or process. Current technology tools can now make the average employee into what media pundit Thomas Freidman calls the "super empowered individual." While at the outset of the twentieth century a large group of workers were virtually powerless, at the outset of the twenty-first century, one or a small group of employees now have the technology-enhanced creative powers to alter an industry or the world for that matter.

CREATIVE DIMENSIONS

According to the Latin Dictionary, *genius* can be defined as the superior or divine nature which is innate in everything, the spiritual part, spirit.[128] A more contemporary description of *genius* is stated as "the individual instance of a general divine nature that is present in every individual person, place, or thing."[129] The Oxford Dictionaries defines genius as "a person who is exceptionally intelligent or creative, either generally or in some particular respect."[130] The idea of genius according to the Encyclopedia Americana is described as a

> personal force and energy of an extremely high order, usually leading to outstanding achievement . . . . Men and women of genius are vehicles for the transformation of society. They create new forms in all the ways in which human will and intellectual power may be expressed: in art, letters, mathematics, science, invention, exploration, economics, philosophy, religion, law, social institutions, politics and war. Often in creating the new, genius downgrades or destroys the old.[131]

---

[128] A Latin Dictionary. Founded on Andrews' edition of Freund's Latin dictionary. Revised, enlarged, and in great part rewritten by Charlton T. Lewis, Ph.D. and. Charles Short, LL.D. Oxford. Clarendon Press. 1879.

[129] Lewis, Charlton T.; Short, Charles (2009). "genius." *A Latin Dictionary*. Meford: Perseus Digital Library, Tufts University. Web. 25 Jan 2013. (http://www.perseus.tufts.edu/cgi-in/ptext?doc=Perseus%3Atext%3A19 99.04.0059%3Aentry%3D%2319459).

[130] "Genius." The Oxford Dictionaries. Oxford:. Oxford University Press. Web. 1 Jan 2013. (Available at: http://oxforddictionaries.com/us/ definition/american_english/genius)

[131] "Genius." Encyclopedia Americana. Web. 23 April 2014. (http://www. britannica.com/EBchecked/topic/229159/genius).

This latter definition of genius addresses the multidimensional areas that are generally initiated and developed by the liberal arts and sciences curricula. Echoes of Schumpeter's creative destruction construct also resonate above with the new genius destroying the old, presumably to make room for new and better products, services, and ideas. While genius is related to creativity, it is not always necessary for achieving transformation, or improvements, in society.

SOCRATES AND CREATIVITY

We might wonder why bringing Socrates into the conversation on creativity is important. But we must recall the example of a philosopher employing his or her greatest tool not only for critical thinking but also for creative thinking. That tool is, again, the *question*. Quite often, the only thing necessary to initiate the creative juices is to simply ask a question, such as: how can we *improve* this process, tool, institution, or situation? Correctly understood, an improvement occurs as a result of a novel, or necessary, input that enhances or increases the level of excellence of a process, tool, or institution. Most improvements do not occur in isolation but as a result of cooperation and dialogue between individuals dedicated to constructing a new reality that serves to solve problems or create new possibilities. As such, what is understood to be a Socratic learning environment tends to initiate and sustain creative thinking propensities and solutions. Below in Figure 1, the Socratic Learning Cycle for Critical and Creative Thinking projects a comprehensive and integrative thinking process that can enable a group of individuals to engage in a productive creative learning process.

Figure 1: Socratic Learning Cycle for Critical/Creative Thinking

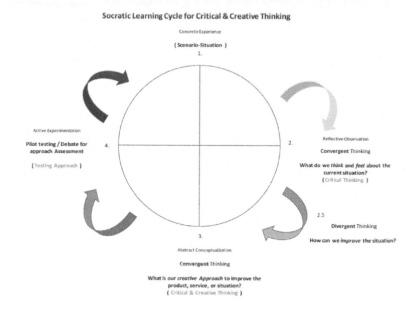

The learning cycle above is an extension of Socratic learning methods, David Kolb's experiential learning cycle, and convergent and divergent thinking theory. Based on my own teaching experience connecting critical thinking methods with creative thinking approaches for better innovation, this model has proven to be very effective. Thus, the Socratic Learning Cycle for Critical and Creative Thinking can be understood in the following way.

We begin at the top with a *concrete experience*, which can be a lecture, a demonstration, or an incident in the environment. In our case, we will assume that a group of professionals working in the design and engineering department at ACME Auto Company has recommended a massive recall due to faulty front-wheel brake systems; basically, the two front-wheel brakes on a late SUV model become inoperable during the summer time and, usually, when the temperature outside rises above 90 degrees. Next, a group of peers in the design and engineering function engages in *reflective observation* about this serious safety problem. The simple question

163

of *what do we think and feel about this situation* initiates the brainstorming session where there are no right or wrong answers, and all responses to the question are documented. The tools of critical thinking, intellectual standards and intellectual traits, are employed during this process to understand the problem and its implications as best as possible.

Next, the group will move into a divergent thinking phase wherein the simple question is asked: *how can we improve this faulty front brake situation in our late SUV model, the Xi?* The focus here is on improving the technology and system, not simply eliminating the problem; it can be assumed that a problem may be removed or "fixed" but not necessarily improve the brakes and other relevant parts of the system. Again, every group member is required to posit an answer to this question, and it is documented; thus, we have a multitude of new ideas with the potential to inform the ultimate solution.

This process then moves into the *abstract conceptualization* phase. In this phase, the group returns to convergent thinking where the question is asked: *what is our creative approach to solving this problem of the faulty front brake system on the SUV model?* Again, the creative solution not only fixes the main problem but also addresses potential related systemwide weaknesses. The particular ideas put forward by each group team member are considered as relevant pieces of a puzzle that, when put together, may look completely unexpected in the end.

One of the ideas posited by an engineer during phase two was submitted as a question. *Are there ways the brake pads can be used to keep the brake system cooler during the summer months and warm during the winter season?* New brake pad materials are designed and developed, and the brake system components are reconfigured.

The process then moves into the final phase, *active experimentation.* Pilot testing is accomplished within the relevant climate conditions around the globe. Results are measured against criteria initially established before testing that would help engineers begin to understand and see whether or not the idea, or hypothesis, of different brake pad material and brake system reconfiguration was viable as an innovation; indeed, to solve the safety issue of the two front-wheel brakes on the SUV model Xi becoming inoperable during the summer time and when the temperature outside rose above 90 degrees Fahrenheit.

Only after the customer and independent auto industry appraisers test and agree that there has been an improvement in brake safety on the Xi will we know if this creative idea worked to solve this real world problem. In fact, the idea of applying creative thinking is also very much related to thinking ethically, or the efforts of achieving justice for customers and society as a whole. We turn to that discussion next.

CHAPTER 7

THINKING ETHICALLY: FOR SOCIAL JUSTICE

Intelligence plus character—that is
the goal of true education.

—Martin Luther King Jr.

🦉 🦉 🦉

Most meaningful discussions about ethics will invariably center on descriptive and normative values; simply stated, these two values categories describe *what is* and recommend what *should be* with regards to thinking that resolves important dilemmas. Ethics can be described as moral principles that govern the lives of an individual or group. *Ethics*, often associated with moral philosophy, can be generally defined as "the discipline dealing with what is good and bad and with moral duty and obligation."[132] Moreover, the Encyclopedia of Psychology defines *ethics* as "the standards that members of a profession must follow."[133] Thus, ethics can be considered an academic discipline, involve moral principles, and inform professional standards that govern work in teaching, the military, medicine, architecture design, welding, or other

---

[132] Ethics. Merriam-Webster Dictionary (2013). Available at: http://www.merriam-webster.com/dictionary/ethics
[133] Encyclopedia of Psychology, Vol 8. Ian E. Kazdin, PhD, Editor-in-Chief. March 2000.

occupational fields; thus, it has been my experience that the liveliest dialogical learning experiences occur with this diverse disciplinary field.

In an article titled *What is ethics?*, four scholars attempt to define *ethics* in a comprehensive "real world" fashion. They write:

> What, then, is ethics? Ethics is two things. First, ethics refers to well-founded standards of right and wrong that prescribe what humans ought to do, usually in terms of rights, obligations, benefits to society, fairness, or specific virtues. Ethics, for example, refers to those standards that impose the reasonable obligations to refrain from rape, stealing, murder, assault, slander, and fraud. Ethical standards also include those that enjoin virtues of honesty, compassion, and loyalty. And, ethical standards include standards relating to rights, such as the right to life, the right to freedom from injury, and the right to privacy. Such standards are adequate standards of ethics because they are supported by consistent and well-founded reasons.
>
> Secondly, ethics refers to the study and development of one's ethical standards. As mentioned above, feelings, laws, and social norms can deviate from what is ethical. So it is necessary to constantly examine one's standards to ensure that they are reasonable and well-founded. Ethics also means, then, the continuous effort of studying our own moral beliefs and our moral conduct, and striving to ensure that we, and the institutions we help to shape, live up to standards that are reasonable and solidly-based.[134]

---

[134] Manuel Velasquez, Claire Andre, Thomas Shanks, S.J., and Michael J. Meyer. *Issues in Ethics* IIE V1 N1 (Fall 1987).

We see that most discussions about ethics can involve the standards that inform rights, obligations, consequences of our actions, and personal virtue. Thus, we have what is called deontological ethics wherein the rights of a person or citizen should not be violated by the group or community, for instance, the right to privacy. Deontological ethics is also understood as a rules-based construct such as the Silver Rule and Golden Rule. The Silver Rule resembles the Hippocratic Oath of doing no harm, but in essence, this rule demands that we *not do* unto others what we would not have others do unto us; and the Golden Rule, often related to the ethics of reciprocity, demands that we *do* unto others what we would have them do unto us. Immanuel Kant's Categorical Imperative serves as the secular version of the Golden Rule, with the exception that he asks us to consider the implications of our actions as being applied universally.

The other ethical construct is called teleological or consequentialist ethics. In the latter construct, the potential or actual consequences of an action will determine whether or not we should move forward with it; if we do commit the action, it is considered ethical usually by a group of rational persons. John Stuart Mill's utilitarian principle often applies here.

In this principle, the best management or political decision is one where the greatest happiness or satisfaction is achieved for the greatest number of people. Obviously, many problems can also develop in practice with this kind of ethics principle. For instance, through a democratic voting process where the majority decision at the poll rules, a majority race or religious group can use its political power to oppress or discriminate against smaller racial or religious groups in their society; thus, the idea of *majority rule* with *minority rights* must be considered in order to employ democratic tools in more ethical ways. If not, then a minority with legitimate claims for justice may be forced to negative or violent means to overturn the outcome of a legitimate political tool, that of the vote. The ethical democratic idea of majority rule coupled with minority rights is especially important for use in new and emerging democracies around the globe.

The third ethical construct is called virtue ethics. Aristotle is the foundation for this construct and it involves the application of human character traits like temperance, prudence, courage, justice, and even fairness. Philosopher John Rawls posits an ethical theory called *fairness as justice*. In his ideas about how to attempt not simply the greatest good for the greatest number of people but fairness for all, one must assume the *veil of ignorance* about who we are; what rights, privileges, and power we have based on our roles as a manager or employee; or our racial background as Whites, Blacks, Asians, Latinos, or Native persons or others. If we deliberate from a position of ignorance about our place of privilege, or lack of it, what kind of decisions would we make at work, in society, or at the ballot box that would, obviously, affect myself and others? Thus, the attempt here is to achieve fairness for all, not just the greatest number who may have disproportionate advantages in society already.

POLITICS, RELIGION, AND ETHICS

Many have argued that legal and religious education should be sufficient to inform better ethical thinking and personal commitment to social justice in our world. Oftentimes, many politically and religiously based educational curricula addressing ethical and social justice themes contain built-in biases in favor of only their adherents. Instead, knowing what kind of just society we would like to live in, which begins with a commitment to protecting individual human conscience and thinking, can inform much of what our secular educational institutions ought to educate for. In a guide entitled *Ethics for the New Millennium*, His Holiness the Dalai Lama writes that twenty-first century ethics principles should be based

> on universal rather than religious principles. It rests on
> the observation that those whose conduct is ethically
> positive are happier and more satisfied and the belief

> that much of the unhappiness we humans endure
> is actually of our own making. Its ultimate goal is
> happiness for every individual, irrespective of religious
> belief.[135]

Thus, it seems that, according to the Dalai Lama, universal principles, those that consider all of humanity's ideas on positive and good conduct, can inform a harmonized system of ethical beliefs that most humans can consider, accept, and assimilate for themselves if they so choose. And effort can be made to encourage ethical behaviors not based on religious manipulation, threats, or incentives about a possible afterlife but simply on good-faith sentiment and thinking about others. Mature types of ethical thinking should be characterized as the kind of reasoning which has excluded personal unfounded biases, prejudicial thoughts for those that are different, favoritism for our own kind, and discriminatory policies against others. Justice, then, begins with the individual thinking ethically, meaning thinking about and actually making decisions that are just for herself and others. Just decisions not only take into account what mores, rules, and laws currently exist, but also what we *should do* to essentially make necessary progress in society.

ETHICAL THINKING FOR SOCIAL JUSTICE

It would be the theme of justice that would initiate the first dialogue in Plato's Republic and still continue to this day. To be *just* can be defined as the quality of being fair and reasonable. Merriam-Webster formally defines the idea of justice as "the principle or ideal of just dealing or right action" or, more specifically, "conformity to truth, fact, or reason." Oftentimes, being fair and reasonable can

---

[135] Study Guide for Ethics for the New Millennium by His Holiness the Dalai Lama. Redwood City, CA: The Dalai Lama Foundation, March 2004, p. 2.

be a relative concept and based on who holds the upper hand in a situation. Thrasymachus would posit as much when responding to Socrates's question about what justice was; the former would argue forcefully that it was rulers who hold formal power, or considered to be strong, in society who defined and determined what is just. But Socrates would point out to Thrasymachus and others that fallible rulers often make laws that turn out not be even in their best interest after all; this could prove disastrous to those who hold power and for those who are attempting to receive due justice through a flawed justice system.

As such, in order for impartial justice to protect the strong and weak in society, the design and development of the "rules of the game" in society must be subject to necessary review and reassessment for their wisdom, soundness, and relevance as an act of ethical legal process. Immanuel Kant's Categorical Imperative, again, meaning that we not commit any action that we would not want applied universally to both strong and weak, informs the designs of justice generally. As a nineteenth century Romantic, Kant appeals not only to our reason but also to our emotions when advancing his ethical maxim.

But I think we must know when to apply limits even to Kant's seeming noble ethics construct as it may become necessary in our mostly grey world to break a strict rule, such as the one to never utter a lie. The usual example used to make this point involves questions such as, *what if the Nazis came to your door looking for Jews during WW II? Would you tell them that you had Jews in your secret cellar or lie to them in the effort to save human lives?* While there is no guarantee that the Nazis, regardless of the Gentile's response, will not kill *all* of the residents, applying instead the ethical construct which recommends that we commit a lesser evil, in this case lying to the Nazis, to prevent a greater one, at worst a massacre, seems to be one of the options to consider initially; there are never easy answers when the extreme abuse of power is involved. Kant's philosophy also included the idea that we view individuals not as means to others' or our ends but as ends in themselves. Does this mean, then, that if we don't lie, we are, in effect, treating the Jews we have now exposed to the Nazis as means to our ends, meaning our goal of never to violate the strict rule of never to lie to others? While it was important for Kant to enfranchise intuition or our emotions as a valid kind of influence on our thinking, it can get tricky for many who are or have been placed within the "outed" or, in the worst case, hated categories in society. Indeed, as our second definition of justice above conveys, just actions must conform to ideas of "facts and reason," not emotion, superstition, racial or gender allegiances, or raw power.

One only has to refer to the results and benefits of DNA evidence for those wrongly accused and convicted to prison to fully appreciate this point; instead, basing justice on dialectical processes involving facts of the case, the tools of critical reasoning, and empirical evidence during a legal trial tends to produce better, not perfect justice. Most individuals operating within the American legal system are aware of how in the Old World church and state authorities were very willing to invoke superstitious ideas or arbitrary rules to determine justice in most legal cases involving common and/or illiterate human beings.

DNA FOR INALIENABLE RIGHTS

Indeed, in the New World, the U.S. *Declaration of Independence* established the essential philosophical and ethical criteria for better justice declaring that "these truths to be *self evident* that all men are created equal . . ." But unbeknownst to many, it was in the Old World during the seventeenth century wherein the seeds of this idea were planted; the idea of inalienable rights was established by a little known Spanish Jesuit. According to Robert J. Spitzer, S.J.:

> The principle of justice reached both its bedrock and flourishing in the principle of natural rights, which originated with a seventeenth century Spanish Jesuit, Francisco Suarez, in a 1610 tractate entitled *De Legibus* (*On the Laws*). Since Suarez was the most widely read

among the Scholastic philosophers of his day, it is reasonable to assume that John Locke and other legal theorists of Locke's time were familiar with Suarez's breakthrough discovery, . . . Locke influenced Thomas Jefferson, who placed Locke's inalienable rights theory within the Declaration of Independence: We hold these truths to be self-evident, that all men are created equal, that they are endowed by their Creator with certain inalienable Rights.[136]

Suarez was instrumental in establishing the idea that the individual human being was *born with* inherent rights, not only with rights conferred by an *external* authority through important documents like the Bill of Rights; the Declaration of Independence established rights including life, liberty, and the pursuit of happiness. Spitzer further writes:

We can see the faint outline of Jefferson's three inalienable rights in this passage—Suarez's right to the self-preservation corresponding to Jefferson's right to life, Suarez's right to the natural perfection of human nature corresponding to Jefferson's right to liberty, and Suarez's right to happiness corresponding to Jefferson's right to the pursuit of happiness.[137]

That truths which humans must consider and abide by be "self evident," or obvious to the rational individual or a jury of our peers, certainly raised the standard of proof or argument for those attempting to persuade others about the rightness of an idea, decision, or policy; if other forms of arbitrary and capricious criteria are used, then a miscarriage of justice will inevitably occur for society as a whole.

---

[136] Spitzer Robert J. *Ten Universal Principles: A Brief Philosophy of the Life Issues.* San Francisco: Ignatius Press, 2011, p. 52. Print.
[137] Ibid. p. 74.

ETHICS, JUSTICE, AND BELIEF

Thus, it is reasonable to assume that normative ethics must inform most of our efforts at building and sustaining the just society; by 'normative" we mean how one *ought* to act to be moral or just. In 1851, Daniel Webster would borrow his first sentence below from Voltaire but add his own ideas of what higher purposes justice serves in our complex world. He writes:

> Justice, sir, is the great interest of man on earth. It is the ligament which holds civilized beings and civilized nations together. Wherever her temple stands, and so long as it is duly honored, there is a foundation for social security, general happiness, and the improvement and progress of our race. And whoever labors on this edifice with usefulness and distinction, whoever clears its foundations, strengthens its pillars, adorns its entablatures, or contributes to raise its august dome still higher in the skies, connects himself, in name, and fame, and character, with that which is and must be as durable as the frame of human society.[138]

Webster uses terms such as *foundation, edifice, pillars, august dome,* and *durable* to create concrete images in our minds, which suggest that the initiation and advancement of justice is the noblest of construction projects necessary for building and sustaining social security and human harmony in society. His high-minded words remind us about how philosophical discourses on justice can also continue to serve as part of the dialogues that bring unlikely "civilized beings and civilized nations" together. Indeed, it would be philosophy that would create the dialogical template wherein groups of diverse individuals could discuss and argue within the

---

[138] Webster, Daniel.On Mr. Justice Story. Edited by Edward Everett, *The Works of Daniel Webster, Boston: 1851, 300.*

social context the most pressing issues involving just actions among human beings on earth.

Many times, philosophical discourse on the idea of demanding swift justice ignores the need to balance the application of proportional justice for the greater good against justice for the individual; oftentimes, a form of self-righteous or vigilante calls for justice fail to factor in that we are all fallible beings and will probably require both justice and mercy at some time in our complicated lives. The movie titled *12 Angry Men* (1957) starring Henry Fonda addresses this point very cogently. In this movie about a jury trial, the accused was not only a product of bad socio-economic conditions but also subject to racist stereotypes in the jury room as part of due process; in the end, it took a Socratic dialogical discourse process lead by Henry Fonda to question and discredit personal biases and prejudiced thinking that were corrupting justice in the this jury room. Thus, justice in society requires not simply the enforcement of just laws, however flawed they may be at certain times, but constructed and enacted in such a way that prevents unethical thinking and feeling when they are considered and applied. Philosophers have attempted to address and clarify moral philosophy that can be applied fairly to complicated dilemmas, especially when it was necessary to assign clear moral responsibility to someone for a moral failure or heinous crimes.

Philosophers, legal scholars, and even religious leaders have attempted to establish more concrete objective criteria and arguments for assigning moral responsibility to humans' actions, and this involves basic philosophical debate addressing free will, knowledge versus ignorance, human sanity, and genetics. So what does a basic philosophical argument addressing the issue of assigning responsibility for seemingly free will acts on the part of individuals, even animals in some cases, look like?

ETHICS, KNOWLEDGE, AND GENETICS

The arguments about whether or not, and for what reasons, human beings can be held morally responsible for their actions has been debated for a very long time in the fields of philosophy, law, ethics, and theology. During the modern and postmodern eras, Rousseau and contemporary philosophers would inform this important topic using various concepts to make their case. Susan Wolf has done the same but also has informed her thinking and writing about free-will and sanity with the ideas of others, including Stace, Frankfurt, and Taylor.

To begin addressing this issue, I need to connect Rousseau's work with Wolf's.[139] Modern-era philosopher Jean-Jacques Rousseau posited important ideas about humans' free will by outlining the similarities and differences between humans and animals. Contemporary French philosopher Luc Ferry writes that, for Rousseau, "animals clearly possessed intelligence, sensibility, even the faculty of communication" but are, nonetheless, guided by instinct as it relates to their natural decisions. However, Ferry writes that "Rousseau came to locate the difference in terms of man's liberty of action, what he called 'perfectibility'—broadly speaking, the capacity to improve oneself over the course of a lifetime";[140] Rousseau's concepts of perfectibility seems to echo in the writings of Wolf. She argues that as adults are different from "dumb animals, infants, and machines," most individuals with the ability to acquire knowledge and evaluation skills to apply to dilemmas have a greater ability to course correct in and over their lives.

Wolf says that we are *free* in the sense required for moral responsibility even if our decisions and characters are *ultimately* determined by factors external to us. She introduces the criteria of sanity and writes:

---

[139] Susan Wolf, Freedom Within Reason (Oxford: Oxford University Press, 1990), Chapter 2.

[140] Luc Ferry. A Brief History of Thought: A Philosophical Guide to Living. Harper Perennial. New York, NY. p. 105

Being sane, we are able to understand and evaluate our characters in a reasonable way, to notice what there is reason to hold on to, what there is reason to eliminate, and what, from a rational and reasonable standpoint, we may retain or get rid of as we please. Being able as well to govern our superficial selves by our deep selves, then, we are able to change the things we find there is reason to change. This being so, it seems that although we may not be *metaphysically* responsible for ourselves—for, after all, we did not create ourselves from nothing—we are *morally* responsible for ourselves, for we are able to understand and appreciate right and wrong, and to change our characters and our actions accordingly.

Her reference to "our deep selves" refers to what she calls the *Real Self View* of moral responsibility, a subset of an individual's deeper psychological makeup. Wolf suggests that we apply the standard of *sanity*, what she calls the Sane Deep Self, to determine moral responsibility. She defines *sane* in this context as simply the ability to know right from wrong or, in a specialized sense, "the ability cognitively and normatively to understand and appreciate the world for what it is"; a sane individual can know *what is* and *what ought to be* in the world generally.

According to Wolf, not having the knowledge of right and wrong prevents individuals from drawing from their deep selves the "resources and reasons that might have served as a basis for self-correction." Thus, when it can be determined that an individual has been reasonably trained, educated, or culturally indoctrinated about a relevant situation requiring action, then it seems reasonable to hold such a person accountable, at some level, for the action's consequences. There are, however, some exceptions to highlight.

EXCEPTIONS TO THE RULE

As it relates to knowledge, complete illiteracy and even an inability to write has often been used as justification to exempt an individual from certain moral responsibilities. For instance, once it is proven that a woman has been prevented from accessing basic formal education in her community, it is reasonable to conclude that she may not be held morally responsible for some actions requiring the ability to read and understand legal content. In cases pertaining to income tax evasion involving literate citizens, the courts have ruled that "the proliferation of statutes and regulations has sometimes made it difficult for the average citizen *to know* and *comprehend* the extent of the duties and obligations imposed by the tax laws" (emphasis mine).

Second, often, there are biological reasons for exempting an individual from moral responsibility for their seeming free-will actions. For example, in the case of a man suffering from Tourette's syndrome, where his profanity toward another in open public creates real harm, science has determined that this man is not acting freely as he is instead reacting to a genetically inherited defect that force actions beyond his ability to control. In the case above pertaining to illiteracy, there is opportunity for correction or perfectibility but not much in the latter case involving a genetic disorder, especially in cases where the individual is unable to afford expensive medical treatment or drugs.

It seems that Wolf makes a very good case for assigning moral responsibility if an individual that can demonstrate a form of reasoned sanity. While it may be difficult to determine moral responsibility for a person's actions, the concept of "perfectibility," achieved through formal education, training, or cultural indoctrination, can be a way to certify a credible ability to know right or wrong in many circumstances and this in light of the fact that many of the influences informing our actions arguably are determined. Wolf writes, "We are able to change the things we find there is reason to change . . . we are *morally* responsible for ourselves, for we are able to understand and appreciate right and wrong, and to change our characters and our actions accordingly." Thus, our characters are improved over time, enhancing also the possibility of being held legally and morally responsible for our seeming free will actions.

Interestingly, Theodore Roosevelt once said, "To educate a man in mind and not in morals is to educate a menace to society." The process of liberal education attempts to educate the man and woman about what is true and what is false, and why; what is generally wrong and what is right, and why. But in order for this process to be more complete, an educational process must also help the individual develop practical competencies in *how to* apply the normative values and rules for the betterment of self and society within the ever expanding circle in the cosmos.

Epilogue

*I know that I am intelligent, because
I know that I know nothing.*

—Socrates

The alarms about the demise of the liberal arts and humanities curricula in American higher education have not subsided as we enter the second decade of the twenty-first century. The often-heard laments include warnings from the academy's philosophy and humanities faculty about the negative effects upon society as a whole when its citizens, the elites in particular, have not engaged at a credible level in the curricula fit for "philosopher kings" or queens. Indeed, within the public school sector, similar alarms have for some time been ringing about the defunding of arts and music programs.

To many, the barbarians are at the gate once again threatening to take our society into a new dark age where, at best, enlightened self-interest and market-based curricula, not religious superstition, eclipse the need for critical reasoning, cultural and economic engagement, and spiritual nourishment within the multipolar postmodern world. These contemporary John the Baptists crying in the wilderness do see the value of a market economy where profits with purpose can be pursued more so than what has been the case thus far; we want to operate in a more ethical free-market economic system but not necessarily live in a market society where human

181

pursuits are undertaken solely for some type of profit, however necessary the latter might be for organizational reinvestment strategies.

Philosopher and legal scholar Martha Nussbaum at the University of Chicago argues that marginalizing a liberal arts education in society, with its emphasis on critical reasoning or appreciation for what is different, prevents the citizens of a nation, often experiencing very good gross national product levels, from questioning environmental pollution or the unjust social and political institutions that retard efforts to democratize how influence is exercised or that continue to disenfranchise "different" groups, women, and the poor. It is tempting to at once accuse Nussbaum and others of imposing Western centric values of justice onto non-Western societies by implying that we must either mind our own business or tolerate the "other's" culture in their suppression of women, religious and ethnically different groups, and new economic competitors; after all, don't we in the West tolerate a level of exploitation of women in the film and entertainment industries or undocumented individuals from all over the world in the workplace?

As the intellectual descendants of the Socratic school of philosophy, many more postmodern philosophers, intellectuals, and educators must consider venturing away from their cloistered Ivy spaces, where only philosophers debate society's central issues among themselves, and once again engage Socratically in the larger sociological contexts asking the relevant and informed wisdom questions. Indeed, there is opportunity to connect both speculative and practical philosophies for new application in the social domain, and it is hoped that a new generation of free citizens can begin to perceive the ongoing relevance of the perennial ideas and philosophies that can still inform daily life. These wisdom questions also can address the deeper multidimensional aspects of life away from the academy where human beings in the real world interact with their daily challenges or, as Kelsey stated, "the problems of real life."

Quite often, higher levels of liberal and professional learning offered within the more developed type of society involve mainly formal training, education, and professional development that initiate and advance individuals' interdisciplinary understanding of the sociological, technological, ecological, economic, political, and ethical (STEEPE) dimensions of the world around us. This interdisciplinary approach should develop in learners understanding about a society's diverse groups, social interactions, and their relationships to various public and private sector institutions that are crucial for open democratic societies: how access and use of available technology-enhanced tools can improve or threaten life, liberty, privacy, and the pursuit of personal and professional goals; how plants and animal kingdoms as nonhuman species must be understood, respected, utilized, and/or preserved for the enhancement of life and health on earth; how the process of production and distribution of goods and services can be accomplished by a mission to serve human needs first, earn profits expected in longer time frames and not shorter ones, where pressure on managers and workers tend to produce more unethical decisions, if not degraded health and family life; how the exercise of political power and influence in society should be informed by normative ethics and a genuine sense of serving first the public interest and the enforcement of just laws; and how human rights advocacy can serve to create, inform, and sustain social, educational, and political practices that are not simply moral and legal, but ethical in nature. The STEEPE analysis and evaluation framework can also enable a group of learners or policy makers to understand, for instance, poverty's sociological, technosocial, ecological, economic, political, and ethical dimensions; thus, there is potential to craft better policy with a more broad and comprehensive understanding of the critical issues causing and affecting poverty.

The necessary balancing and tensions between the need to think critically and appreciate the beauty and complexities of the human experience, in addition to empowering others to ethically innovate and enhance a society's social and economic well-being, are clearly some of the chief challenges for global leaders in and out of higher education during the twenty-first century. And yet a misunderstanding of how ancient and human-centered forms of learning can still create understanding about today's complex human realities prevents many postmoderns from seriously considering how a liberal education can still inform questions and answers to contemporary dilemmas; this also includes helping struggling regions of the world develop in better ways.

LIBERAL ARTS AND SCIENCES FOR
THE ISLAMIC CIVILIZATION

At this point in history, we find ourselves in the higher learning community praising some of Asian countries' decisions to infuse a level of liberal education into some of their institutions of higher learning. Many parts of Africa have used liberal learning to achieve independence from repressive and exploitive regimes based in and out of this part of the world. These developments are important, especially as the West recovers from its crisis of legitimacy, but due to its expertise in higher learning, continues to serve as a partner and advocate of the liberal learning education model, which ultimately extends the human emancipation project throughout the world; and this includes our old friends in the Islamic world.

As was discussed earlier in the book, it was scholars from the Islamic civilization who infused advanced medical education into Europe at the medical school of Salerno (circa ninth century AD) and the critical ideas of Aristotle and other philosophers within Andalusian Spain during the twelfth century and subsequently helping the West climb out of the Dark Ages. Thus, we must return the favor to the Islamic civilization as it is during this time in its history that conspiracy thinking is at its worst, contributing to its underdevelopment and seeming culture of violence and war. Efforts to reintroduce the idea of the liberal arts and humanities to the Islamic world are already under way, as in the example of Zaytuna College in Berkeley, California. Their mission statement reads,

> Zaytuna College seeks to educate and prepare morally committed professional, intellectual, and spiritual leaders who are grounded in the Islamic scholarly tradition and conversant with the cultural currents and critical ideas shaping modern society.[141]

While the language used to develop this mission statement seems vague at some levels, it seems the institution is nonetheless committed to engaging the critical ideas shaping ours and their "modern society." There are no references here of returning to the Golden Age of Islam or of establishing a global caliphate over the world. Indeed, evidence of the Seven Liberal Arts can be discerned within the college's educational philosophy. It states,

> The courses are designed collectively by a diverse faculty who bring unique strengths and perspectives to the conversation. Courses in law speak to concerns in Ethics; discussions in the Qur'an class spill over into astronomy; tensions in the freshman seminar are resolved in a class on spiritual psychology and cosmology; the utility and limits of logic are explored in philosophic theology and the history of science; the power of the imagination is unleashed in literature; the "rise and fall of civilizations" is reassessed through a study of world religions and contemporary Islamic thought; mastery of grammar and rhetoric in English

---

[141] Zaytuna College. Mission Statement. Web. 10 May 2014.

and Arabic propels us through great ideas embedded in
timeless texts.[142]

Thus, we see references to astronomy, logic, grammar, rhetoric, in addition to humanities such as religions, science, literature, cosmology, psychology, and Islamic thought. Many parts of the world, including the developed world, require appropriate forms of liberal learning, indeed, if they intend to adopt a form of free-market democracy that values and honors the individual human being. These nations' citizens then must be equipped to think, analyze, and evaluate for themselves if they are to develop into productive and ethical societies. These intellectual skills are not Western skills, but human skills developed and belonging to all global citizens.

---

[142] Ibid. Bachelor's Program.

Made in the USA
Coppell, TX
21 August 2020